BASEBALL IN TOLEDO

Roger Bresnahan is the only Toledo native son to be enshrined in the National Baseball Hall of Fame. He began his career as a pitcher and appeared briefly for Toledo in 1898 as an 18 year old. He went on to be an outstanding catcher and all round player. He is credited with inventing and using shin guards while playing for the New York Giants. Following his playing days, Bresnahan managed and coached in the major leagues. He was owner of the Toledo team from 1916 through 1923. At Toledo he served as president of the club, and also managed, coached, and played. (National Baseball Hall of Fame and Library, Cooperstown, N.Y.)

BASEBALL IN TOLEDO

John R. Husman

ARCADIA

Published by Arcadia Publishing,
an imprint of Tempus Publishing, Inc.
2 Cumberland Street
Charleston, SC 29401

Printed in Great Britain.

Library of Congress Catalog Card Number: Applied For.

For all general information contact Arcadia Publishing at:
Telephone 843-853-2070
Fax 843-853-0044
E-Mail sales@arcadiapublishing.com

For customer service and orders:
Toll-Free 1-888-313-2665

Visit us on the internet at http://www.arcadiapublishing.com

For Michelle—a model of strength, courage, and faithfulness.
This wonderful woman is an inspiration.

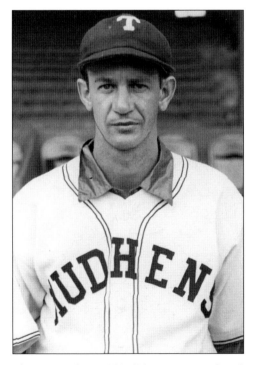

Stan Corbett, Toledo Mud Hens pitcher, 1938. (Photo reprinted with permission of *The Toledo Blade*.)

4

CONTENTS

A car on the Dorr Street line of the Toledo Consolidated Street Railway in about 1910 advertising that baseball will be played that day. This may be one of the extra cars that was put in service on game days to handle baseball crowds. It was about a 12-block walk from Dorr Street and Detroit Avenue to Swayne Field. (Toledo-Lucas County Public Library, Charles F. Mensing photograph.)

ACKNOWLEDGMENTS

THIS BOOK IS POSSIBLE because the owners or guardians of the images it contains have generously shared them. The author wishes to thank especially *The Toledo Blade*, Tom Walton, Editor, and Mary Mackzum, Head Librarian and The Toledo-Lucas County Public Library, Local History and Genealogy Department, Jim Marshall, Manager. Special thanks also to The National Baseball Hall of Fame and Library, Bill Burdick, Manager Photo Services Department and The Toledo Mud Hens, Jason Griffin, Director Media/Public Relations. Gregory Tye, Senior Producer of WGTE Public Broadcasting, has provided invaluable assistance and Bob Koehler made numerous images from his personal collection available.

The author thanks Sandy Husman and Marianne Quellhorst for their numerous reads and edits and constant support.

Finally there are many individuals who have helped with information, or documentation, or supplied images. Taken in total, their contribution is a major one: Brian Britten, Rick Bunge, Bill Carle, Donna Christian, Bill Clark, Karen Cole, Harold Esch, Ken Fenster, Steve Gietschier, Frank Gilhooley, Rex Hamann, Nancy Hawkins, Tom Hill, Reed Howard, Ann Hurley, Jack Husman, Walter Husman, Jerry Jackson, Kim Johns, Jack Kerin, Marilyn Klar, Craig Lammers, Steve Lauer, Ken Levin, Mike Lora, Alyce Lutomski, Chuck Lutomski, Irene Martin, Mike McCardel, Sean McKeown, Jay Miller, Greg Miller, Marc Okkonen, Pete Palmer, John Pardon, Chris Perry, Bob Tiemann, Jim Tootle, Laura Voelz, John Wagner, Jim Weber, and John Widmer.

Additional persons are thanked through picture credits.

INTRODUCTION

THE WHOLE OF TOLEDO professional baseball history seems to fall naturally into several eras. Beginning in 1883, the Early Era continued through the 1901 season. During these formative years, owners, teams, leagues, and parks came and went. Team nicknames included the Blue Stockings, Toledos, Maumees, Black Pirates, White Stockings, and the Swamp Angels. In 1896, Charles Strobel bought the team. Through his efforts, Toledo baseball became a legitimate and stable business in Toledo, and the Mud Hens name was born.

Toledo became a charter member of the American Association (AA), the premier minor league of its time, in 1902. This relationship with seven other midwestern cities remained nearly constant until Toledo dropped out after the 1955 season. Baseball's farm system developed during this time, and the Mud Hens were associated with the Indians, Browns, Tigers, and Braves. Toledo teams were also known as the Soumichers, Iron Men, and Sox during the American Association Era.

There was no professional baseball in Toledo from 1956 through 1964. A community effort led by Ned Skeldon returned the game in 1965. The franchise was entered in the International League and the park was located at a converted racetrack in Maumee, Ohio. During the Maumee Era, the club, once again known as the Mud Hens, was involved in working agreements with the Yankees, Tigers, Phillies, Indians, Twins, and the Tigers again. For the most part, the team floundered, winning just one pennant and one Governor's Cup. Gene Cook became general manager in 1978, and under his leadership fan interest was rekindled and attendance grew. The visionary Cook was the driving force in moving Toledo into the present era.

Toledo's Mud Hens returned home, in 2002, to downtown Toledo. A new park was built in the heart of the city. The Coming Home Era began with the fans shattering attendance records and the Mud Hens winning a championship.

It has been said that it doesn't take a very high flagpole to hold Toledo's pennants. In 106 seasons only six pennants have been won with three of those coming in the nineteenth century, and the last in 1968. Toledo teams have finished in last place more often than any other position, and they are perennially in the second division. On the other hand, there have been some wonderful seasons, some near hits, and some outstanding individual performances. Toledo has had more than its fair share of noteworthy players, managers, and executives. Add to these the native sons who have made their way to baseball's major leagues, and it is sure that Toledo has made a significant impact on our national game.

Toledo's 106th professional baseball season was played in 2002 in the same place as the first one in 1883—on Monroe Street in downtown Toledo. (The Toledo Mud Hens.)

ONE

The Early Era

1883–1901

PROFESSIONAL BASEBALL hit a home run in its inaugural season in Toledo as the Blue Stockings won the Northwestern League pennant over Saginaw. What followed for the remainder of the nineteenth century was chaos. Toledo had teams of seven different names, owned by at least seven different individuals, and played in seven different leagues for ten different managers and in nine different parks. There were four seasons of no baseball at all in Toledo and several more that were not completed.

Toledo's first season success earned it a place in baseball's major leagues. The Toledos were respectable, finishing 8th of the 12 teams in the American Association, which included the nation's largest cities. Workhorse pitcher Tony Mullane set Toledo single season pitching records that still stand, and most certainly always will. Mullane's catcher, Moses Fleetwood "Fleet" Walker, became the first black man to play major league baseball; later in the season, his brother, Welday, became the second. Except for the first few games of the 1883 season, Charlie Morton had managed Toledo for both seasons and proved to be very capable.

Apparently, the major leagues had overextended themselves by playing in 33 cities in 1884. Contraction found Toledo in the Western League in 1885, but not for long. The league suffered financial collapse in less than three months. Toledo did not have baseball again until 1888, when the Ketcham family became interested in baseball and entered the weak Toledo Maumees in the weak Tri-State League.

Charlie Morton returned in 1889 with a strong team he had assembled and played as the Toledo Black Pirates in the International League. Toledo had a winning record and finished fourth. That solid 1889 performance earned Morton and the Black Pirates another shot at the major American Association. Again, Toledo was respectable in the field, but only fair at the gate, and could not sustain the effort into the next season. The Ketchams abandoned the baseball business, and there would be no baseball in Toledo again in 1891.

The 1892 season was yet another disaster. A new edition of Black Pirates was entered in the again ill-fated Western League that folded early in July. Another year devoid of baseball in Toledo followed this abbreviated season. Dennis Long fielded the White Stockings in the reconstituted Western League in 1894 and had some success, finishing second. However, the next season Toledo's blue laws, which forbade Sunday baseball, proved too oppressive for Long. A Sunday gate was promised in Terre Haute, Indiana, and, so, he moved the team west in midseason and called them the Hottentots.

A team known as the Swamp Angels began the 1896 season for Toledo in the Interstate League. Baseball entrepreneur Charles Strobel bought the team in July and personally led it to a second-half championship. He won a pennant the next season as well. He was on his way to making baseball a part of Toledo history. Initially, he sidestepped the blue laws by playing Sunday games outside the city limits, and later helped to have the laws repealed. He built Toledo's first "permanent" park and won a lot of baseball games. Charles Strobel established baseball as a legitimate business in Toledo and gained entry for his team into the new American Association, America's premier minor league.

Year	Team	Finish	W	L	Attendance	League	Manager	Affiliate
1883	Blue Stockings	1 of 8	56	28		Northwestern	Voltz, Morton	
1884	Toledos	8 of 12	46	58	55,000	American Assoc.	Morton	Major
1885	Toledos	5 of 6	9	21		Western	O'Leary	
1888	Maumees	8 of 10	46	64		Tri-State	Smith, Mountain,	
							Woods	
1889	Black Pirates	4 of 8	54	41		International	Morton	
1890	Black Pirates	4 of 8	68	64	70,000	American Assoc.	Morton	Major
1892	Black Pirates	4 of 8	25	24		Western	MacGregor	
1894	White Stockings	2 of 8	67	55		Western	Long	
1895	White Stockings	8 of 8	23	28		Western	Long	
1896	Swamp Angels	2 of 8	39	29		Inter-State	Torreyson	
1896	Mud Hens	1 of 8	47	16		Inter-State	Strobel	
1897	Mud Hens	1 of 8	83	43		Inter-State	Strobel	
1898	Mud Hens	2 of 8	84	68		Inter-State	Strobel	
1899	Mud Hens	3 of 8	82	58		Inter-State	Strobel	
1900	Mud Hens	3 of 8	81	58		Inter-State	Strobel	
1901	Mud Hens	3 of 8	77	60		Western	Strobel	

TOLEDO NORTHWESTERN LEAGUE CHAMPION CLUB—1883

The 1883 Blue Stockings, Toledo's first professional team, won the Northwestern League pennant. Home games were played at League Park on the north side of Monroe Street, between Thirteenth and Fifteenth Streets. The home team won the first professional baseball game played in Toledo, 5-4, over Bay City on May 5, 1883. The team uniform was blue shirts and stockings with white trousers. From left to right are: (front row) Tom Poorman and Horace Lockwood; (middle row) Sam Moffet, Sam Barkley, manager Charlie Morton, Curt Welch, and Hank O'Day; (back row) Joe Miller, Jack Jones, Fleet Walker, Chappy Lane, and John Tilley. (Toledo-Lucas County Public Library, Ralph Lin Weber collection.)

Noah H. Swayne, Jr. was a member of the Board of Directors of Toledo's first professional baseball club in 1883. He maintained life long involvement in Toledo professional baseball and was a director of numerous Toledo clubs. Swayne himself was a notable athlete, a sportsman from his youth, and played top flight amateur baseball. A landmark Toledo ballpark, Swayne Field, would be named for him. (Photo reprinted with permission of *The Toledo Blade*.)

11

The 1884 Toledo Toledos was the first team to represent the city in a major league. This photograph, represented to have been taken at the Tri-State Fairgrounds at Dorr Street and Upton Avenue, is actually a mock-up taken with the players standing in front of a "set." The club was also purported to have played weekend and holiday games at the fairgrounds, but research reveals that the Toledos never played there, though amateur teams did. Home games were played at League Park on Monroe Street. Noticeably missing from the picture are two black players, Moses and Welday Walker, the first of their race to play in the major leagues. They were not alone, however, as only 12 of the 21 players who appeared in the Toledo lineup that year are present. From left to right are: (front row) Joe Miller, player and manager Charlie Morton, Deacon McGuire, and Tug Arundel; (back row) Frank Olin, Chappy Lane, Curt Welch, Sam Barkley, Tony Mullane, Hank O'Day, George Meister, and Tom Poorman. (Toledo-Lucas County Public Library, Ralph Lin Weber collection.)

12

Shown here in his 1883 Toledo Baseball Club uniform, Moses Fleetwood "Fleet" Walker was the first black man to play major league baseball. As catcher for Toledo's 1884 entry in the then major league American Association, he preceded the noted Jackie Robinson by 63 seasons. The previous year, Walker played for Toledo's championship entry in the Northwestern League. His brother Welday Wilberforce Walker also played for Toledo in 1884. (Toledo Lucas-County Public Library, Ralph Lin Weber collection.)

Charlie Morton, a journeyman baseball manager, promoter, and player, managed Toledo's first team to a pennant in 1883, managed the 1889 club in the highly competitive International League, and also managed the 1884 and 1890 entries in the major league American Association. During an era when Toledo performance on the field was sporadic, Morton's teams played against the strongest competition and generally had winning results. His winning percentage, based on a 219–180 won-lost record, is second among all Toledo managers. As a player, the then 28 year old played regularly in 1883 as an outfielder and third baseman and was the team's leading hitter with a .335 average. Thereafter he inserted himself in the lineup only occasionally. (Toledo-Lucas County Public Library, Ralph Lin Weber collection.)

Tony Mullane and Hank O'Day were a one-two pitching punch for the 1884 Toledos that played in the major league American Association. Technically, these likenesses from the 1884 team photo are crudely done, but they display a nineteenth-century baseball tradition. In team pictures, the pitcher held the ball. In this case, both are pitchers (both hold a ball) and O'Day displays a bat as well. Between them, they started 105 of Toledo's 110 games that year. Mullane led the way and set all-time Toledo records that still stand with 36 wins, 325 strikeouts, and 567 innings pitched. In all, Mullane pitched 13 major league seasons, winning 284 games. O'Day, who had led the 1883 Toledo Blue Stocking to a pennant, also continued in the major leagues. He pitched six more years and became the first, and one of a very few, to play, manage, and umpire in the major leagues. He was one of the game's great arbiters, working in the National League for 30 seasons. It was O'Day who made the famous Merkle boner call (see page 26). (Toledo-Lucas County Public Library, Ralph Lin Weber collection.)

This full color 24 by 36 inch promotional poster for a Toledo cigar manufacturer not only depicts the 1889 Toledo Black Pirates, their manager, and owner, but also shows Toledo's home season schedule. In the center is the only known image, of any kind, of Speranza Park, the club grounds. Speranza was located near the intersection of Cherry Street and Franklin Avenue, just north of the present site of St. Vincent Mercy Medical Center, and was active from July 4, 1888 through the 1890 season. During the time Speranza Park was in use, the club was owned first by George Ketcham and then his brother, Valentine Ketcham, Jr. The park was named for the family's yacht. Shown in the upper left-hand corner is president Valentine H. Ketcham, Jr., and in the upper right is manager Charlie Morton. Team members starting at the top of the diamond and moving clockwise are Joe Quest, Billy Alvord, Harry Sage, Ed Cushman, Taylor Shaffer, Bill Van Dyke, William Bottenus, John Sneed, Fred Smith, William Wehrle, George Stallings, and Perry Werden. (Transcendental Graphics.)

Harry Sage, the Toledo Black Pirates' catcher in 1889 and 1890, was featured on these early baseball cards that promoted Old Judge cigarettes. Note the padded sliding pants and catcher's protective fielding gloves. The hands apart batting grip was one of several styles used in the nineteenth century. (Library of Congress, Prints and Photographs Division.)

Toledo's nineteenth-century baseball parks, except for Armory Park built in 1897, are lost. They are known to us only through the written newspaper accounts of their time. League Park (1883–1885), on the north side of Monroe Street between Thirteenth and Fifteenth Streets, and Speranza Park (1888–1890), between Cherry Street and Franklin, just north of the present day St. Vincent Mercy Medical Center, were the most prominent and hosted major league Toledo teams. Presque Isle Park (1888) on the east side of the Maumee River, near its mouth; Olympic Park (1892) in the Indiana, Hawley, Woodland area; and near to that, the Ewing Street Park (1894–1896) at Ewing and Pinewood; and Whitestocking Park (1894–1895) on Lagrange Street were shorter lived and less prominent. In addition, Riverside Park (1885) and Casino or Bay View Park (1896–1900) were used for weekend baseball only, usually to avoid Toledo's blue laws. No known photograph of any of these parks exists. And, except for Whitestocking Park, none is shown on a map, plat, or survey. The exception is this 1895 plat of the location of Whitestocking Park by the Sanborn Map Company. The center of the grandstand is located on Lagrange Street, between Hudson and Pearl. (Andrew Sager.)

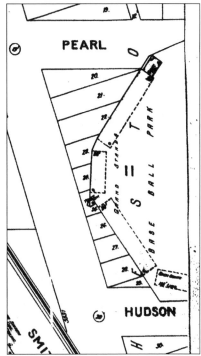

A Toledo professional baseball team first adopted the nickname of Mud Hens during the 1896 season. During that season the team played its Sunday games at Bay View Park, which was outside of the city limits in order to avoid Toledo's blue laws. Large numbers of American Coots (*Fulica Americana*), commonly known as Mud Hens, occupied the nearby marshes. It is from these birds that the team acquired its name. Prior to the Mud Hens name, Toledo teams were known by six different nicknames in nine seasons. Except for two short-term departures, the name has stuck in the 97 seasons and 103 years since. (Washtenaw Audubon Society.)

This Toledo street scene shows Toledo's "financial canyon," and is described as "Young lady in 1896 bicycles to work on Madison Avenue towards Summit Street. The famous Boody House [hotel] is in the left background." (Toledo Lucas-County Public Library.)

The close-up view of the above photograph reveals a banner stretched across Madison Avenue beckoning all to leave work downtown and go to a home game that afternoon. In 1896 baseball was played at the Ewing Street Park during the week. But because of Toledo's blue laws Sunday games were played at Bay View Park, which was outside of the city limits. The Ewing Street Park was in service for three years, from 1894 through 1896, and was located within an area bounded by Ewing Street on the west, Pinewood Avenue (then Missouri) on the south, Hawley Street on the west, and Woodland Avenue (then Wisconsin) on the north. The park was served by four trolley lines and was a 20-minute walk from the business district shown. (Toledo Lucas-County Public Library.)

The 1896 and 1897 teams, the first to be called the Mud Hens, are the only Toledo teams to win consecutive pennants, and narrowly missed a third in 1898. Owner Charles Strobel used these championships to finally and firmly establish baseball as a continuously operating business in Toledo. The 1896 Mud Hens, from left to right, are: (front row) Kid Keenan, Stanley Arthur, and William Hartman; (middle row) Erve Beck, Bill Coyle, president and manager Charles Strobel, George Kelb, and William Smith; (back row) Samuel Vetters, Charlie Ferguson, George Kihm, captain Fred Cooke, and Arthur Van Winkler. (Toledo-Lucas County Public Library, Ralph Lin Weber collection.)

The 1897 Mud Hens, from left to right, are: (front row) Charlie Ferguson, Bob Ewing, John Blue, George Darby, and George Kelb; (middle row) Bade Myers, Stanley Arthur, president and manager Charles Strobel, Bob Langsford, and Jeremiah McDonough; (back row) William Smith, Bill Hassamaer, captain Bob Gilks, Erve Beck, and William Hartman. (Toledo-Lucas County Public Library, Ralph Lin Weber collection.)

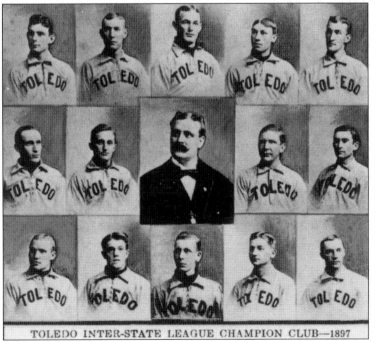

TOLEDO INTER-STATE LEAGUE CHAMPION CLUB—1897

This early photograph of Armory Park, built and opened in 1897, shows the National Guard Armory in left field and St. Mary's Catholic (German) Church, at Cherry and Michigan, just to its right. This may not depict real game action as a catcher is not visible and the player at home plate does not appear to have a bat. Although the construction is somewhat crude, note that advertising already appears on the outfield fences. (See pages 24 and 25 for a later photograph and more details about Armory Park.) (Toledo-Lucas County Public Library.)

This artist's rendition of the downtown Toledo Civic Center area depicts Armory Park in its neighborhood. The drawing, entitled *Civic Center Area Yesterday,* is contained in a project proposal of the Toledo and Lucas County Planning Commissions dated 1943. The park was in service for professional baseball from 1897 until 1909, and for amateur sports and other events for some time after that. The time depicted in this drawing is difficult to determine and may be a composite, but it does show where Armory Park stood in relationship to city streets and other prominent structures. Most notable, of course, is the Ohio National Guard Armory that actually formed the left field wall of the park. (Toledo-Lucas County Plan Commissions.)

Two

The American Association (AA) Era

1902–1955

TOLEDO JOINED WITH COLUMBUS, Louisville, Indianapolis, Milwaukee, Minneapolis, St. Paul, and Kansas City to form the American Association (AA), which began play in 1902. The new American Association played the highest caliber of minor league baseball and was remarkably stable. With one short-lived exception, these eight cities maintained their relationship for half of a century.

Competition in the AA was extremely tough and, generally, Toledo did not fare well. Overall, Toledo won only two pennants, finished in the second division seven out of ten seasons, and finished dead last more often than any other position. Conversely, many fine players wore the Toledo uniform, but not enough of them to provide consistent winning records.

Toledo's American Association Mud Hens began play in downtown Armory Park. After William Armour bought the team in 1907 and managed it to a pair of winning seasons, Armory proved to be too small. Armour raised the capital and built a new park, away from downtown at Monroe Street and Detroit Avenue. The capital may have come from Cleveland's Charlie Somers who owned the Cleveland American League club, and later had an open and visible relationship with Toledo. The land was leased to the team by long time club board member Noah Swayne. When opened in 1909, Swayne Field was as fine and modern a ballpark as there was in the country, and it became the center for outdoor sports in Toledo.

The Mud Hens were moved to Cleveland by Somers for 1914 and 1915 to help keep the expansion Federal League out of that city. After the Federal collapse, Toledoan Roger Bresnahan bought the club and returned it to Toledo for the 1916 season. Initially he called the club the Iron Men and acted as manager and part-time player. With World War I contributing to his troubles, Bresnahan had little success except for a strong finish in 1920, which earned a record Toledo gate. The club floundered until the arrival of Casey Stengel in 1926. Stengel put together a veteran dominated club that won the pennant in 1927, and went on to win the city's only Junior World Series championship in its history. Stengel's magic faded as did the nation's economy and the club went into receivership. Local businessman Waldo Shank took the club on and kept it afloat until he sold it to the Detroit Tigers. The era of the farm system had begun, but Toledo was undersupplied with quality players by both the Browns and again the Tigers, who finally sold the team in 1951. Operating as an independent, the club left for Charleston, West Virginia, midway through the 1952 season. The Braves moved their Milwaukee Brewers club here for 1953. The new club was called the Sox and immediately won Toledo's second American Association pennant. The Sox also won the hearts of Toledo's fans who turned out in record numbers. After two more seasons, the Braves moved their top farm club again, and shortly thereafter Swayne Field was razed. Again, Toledo was without baseball, but this time it would last.

The Negro Leagues were also represented in Toledo during the first half of the twentieth century. The teams were the Tigers of 1923 in the Negro National League, the Crawfords of 1939 in both the Negro National League and Negro American League, and the Cubs who played in the United States League in 1945. The Negro American League and the Negro National League were major leagues while the United States League was a minor league. These teams played at Swayne Field when the American Association team was on the road. Press coverage of Negro League baseball was sporadic and incomplete. Accurate records of these teams and individuals are not available, and no photograph of a Negro League player in a Toledo uniform has yet been found.

Year	Team	Finish	W	L	Attendance	League	Manager	Affiliate
1902	Mud Hens	8 of 8	42	98		American Assoc.	Strobel	
1903	Mud Hens	8 of 8	48	91		American Assoc.	Reisling	
1904	Mud Hens	8 of 8	42	109		American Assoc.	Long, Clingman, Burns	
1905	Mud Hens	7 of 8	60	91		American Assoc.	Finn, Grillo	
1906	Mud Hens	4 of 8	79	69		American Assoc.	Grillo	
1907	Mud Hens	2 of 8	88	65		American Assoc.	Armour	
1908	Mud Hens	4 of 8	81	72	162,009	American Assoc.	Armour	
1909	Mud Hens	6 of 8	80	86	164,051	American Assoc.	Abbott, Seybold	
1910	Mud Hens	2 of 8	91	75	165,935	American Assoc.	Holmes, Hinchman	
1911	Mud Hens	6 of 8	78	86	120,658	American Assoc.	Hinchman	
1912	Mud Hens	2 of 8	98	66	158,338	American Assoc.	Hartsel	
1913	Mud Hens	6 of 8	69	98	104,342	American Assoc.	Hartsel, Bronkie	
1914	Soumichers	3 of 10	43	35		South Michigan	Hartsel	
1914	Soumichers	10 of 10	9	58	0	South Michigan	Hartsel	
1916	Iron Men	6 of 8	78	86	124,363	American Assoc.	Bresnahan	
1917	Iron Men	8 of 8	57	95	98,921	American Assoc.	Bresnahan	
1918	Iron Men	8 of 8	23	54	124,363	American Assoc.	Bresnahan	
1919	Mud Hens	7 of 8	59	91	89,712	American Assoc.	Zeider, Bresnahan	
1920	Mud Hens	3 of 8	87	79	241,718	American Assoc.	Bresnahan	
1921	Mud Hens	7 of 8	80	88	198,148	American Assoc.	Clymer, Luderus	
1922	Mud Hens	7 of 8	65	101	155,631	American Assoc.	Luderus, Whitted	

Year	Team	Finish	W	L	Attendance	League	Manager	Affiliate
1923	Mud Hens	8 of 8	54	114	98,694	American Assoc.	Whitted, Terry	
1923	Tigers					Negro National	Johnson	Major
1924	Mud Hens	5 of 8	82	83	205,658	American Assoc.	Burke	
1925	Mud Hens	6 of 8	77	90	149,299	American Assoc.	Burke	
1926	Mud Hens	4 of 8	87	77	230,610	American Assoc.	Stengel	
1927	Mud Hens	1 of 8	101	67	316,328	American Assoc.	Stengel	
1928	Mud Hens	6 of 8	79	88	182,814	American Assoc.	Stengel	
1929	Mud Hens	8 of 8	67	100	106,021	American Assoc.	Stengel	
1930	Mud Hens	3 of 8	88	66	179,433	American Assoc.	Stengel	
1931	Mud Hens	8 of 8	68	100	80,067	American Assoc.	Stengel	
1932	Mud Hens	4 of 8	87	80	94,210	American Assoc.	Falk	Indians
1933	Mud Hens	3 of 4	70	83	83,890	American Assoc.	O'Neill	
1934	Mud Hens	4 of 4	68	84	61,866	American Assoc.	O'Neill	
1935	Mud Hens	7 of 8	64	86	53,088	American Assoc.	Haney	
1936	Mud Hens	8 of 8	59	92	67,393	American Assoc.	Haney	Tigers
1937	Mud Hens	2 of 8	89	65	259,267	American Assoc.	Haney	Tigers
1938	Mud Hens	5 of 8	79	74	183,192	American Assoc.	Haney	Tigers
1939	Mud Hens	8 of 8	47	107	85,771	American Assoc.	Thomas	Tigers
1939	Crawfords	6 of 7	8	11		Negro National/ American	Charleston	Major
1940	Mud Hens	7 of 8	59	90	86,067	American Assoc.	Taylor	Browns
1941	Mud Hens	5 of 8	82	72	114,823	American Assoc.	Taylor, Haney	Browns
1942	Mud Hens	4 of 8	78	73	110,164	American Assoc.	Haney	Browns
1943	Mud Hens	4 of 8	76	76	102,621	American Assoc.	Fournier	Browns
1944	Mud Hens	2 of 8	95	58	198,870	American Assoc.	Marquart	Browns
1945	Mud Hens	6 of 8	69	84	146,638	American Assoc.	Marquart	Browns
1945	Cubs					U.S. (Negro)	Spencer	
1946	Mud Hens	6 of 8	69	84	234,062	American Assoc.	Detore	Browns
1947	Mud Hens	8 of 8	61	92	169,525	American Assoc.	Snyder	Browns
1948	Mud Hens	7 of 8	61	91	114,310	American Assoc.	Detore	Browns
1949	Mud Hens	8 of 8	64	90	103,712	American Assoc.	Mayo	Tigers
1950	Mud Hens	7 of 8	65	87	88,393	American Assoc.	Mayo	Tigers
1951	Mud Hens	6 of 8	70	82	99,932	American Assoc.	Tighe	Tigers
1952	Mud Hens	8 of 8	46	107	41,497	American Assoc.	Hemsley	
1953	Sox	1 of 8	90	64	343,614	American Assoc.	Holmes, Selkirk	Braves
1954	Sox	6 of 8	74	80	156,989	American Assoc.	Selkirk	Braves
1955	Sox	5 of 8	81	73	182,985	American Assoc.	Selkirk	Braves

CHARLES J. STROBEL,
President Toledo Baseball Club.

Perhaps, for all that he had to do with the development of baseball in Toledo, we should call Charles J. Strobel "The Father of Toledo Baseball." He was owner of the Toledo club from 1896 through 1904, and legitimized baseball as a local business. It was during his tenure that the now world famous Mud Hen nickname was coined. He, along with Mayor Samuel "Golden Rule" Jones, established Sunday baseball within the city. He entered Toledo in the highly competitive American Association, a relationship that lasted more that 50 years. In addition, he may have been the best field manager that Toledo has ever had, winning two pennants, winning consistently, and developing many fine players including Addie Joss, one of baseball's best ever pitchers. But most of all, he had the vision to build a downtown ball park that gave stability and permanence to Toledo baseball. (Toledo-Lucas County Public Library.)

This game action photograph of Armory Park dates from about 1904. Armory Park was Toledo's first permanent park and was home to the Mud Hens from 1897 until 1909. Located downtown on Spielbusch Avenue on the site of the present Federal courthouse, the adjacent National Guard Armory lent its name to the park. The small field was not well suited for showcasing the legging out of triples and inside-the-park home runs or for outfielders chasing down long drives, features of the game at the turn of the century. The right field wall was so close that balls hit

24

Bobby Gilks played more seasons and more games in a Toledo uniform than any other player. He was with Toledo for the 1894–1895 and 1897–1902 seasons, or eight years and 1040 games. An outfielder, he also helped out at first base and shortstop and pitched occasionally as well. With Toledo he batted .297 and twice led his league in hits. Gilks played professional baseball for 26 years, five of them in the major leagues, managed seven minor league seasons, and later was a scout for Connie Mack's Philadelphia American League team. (Toledo Lucas-County Public Library, Ralph Lin Weber collection)

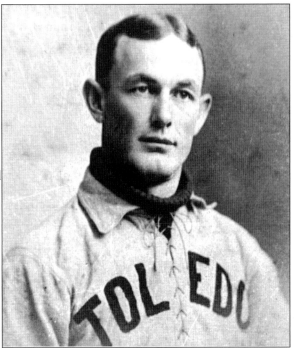

over it were scored as doubles rather than home runs. The seating capacity was also small; the largest crowd was the 6,900 who squeezed in for the first game of the 1906 season. Visible in the background are the steeple of St. Paul's Lutheran Church and the dome of the Lucas County courthouse, both still a part of the Toledo skyline. The canvas to the right is a temporary wall necessary because fire had destroyed the third base grandstand. (Rolf Scheidel.)

Top-notch amateur baseball flourished in Toledo as elsewhere early in the twentieth century, and the Toledo sandlots produced many outstanding players. This image of the Shamrock club was taken in 1905, probably at Toledo's downtown Armory Park. The player at the far left in the top row is the famed New York Giant Fred Merkle. He is unfairly remembered for a huge base running error as a 19-year-old rookie that is known as Merkle's boner, and not his solid 16-year major league career. (Photo reprinted with permission of *The Toledo Blade*.)

The 1905 Toledo Mud Hens are shown here in their spring training headquarters at Paducah, Kentucky. From left to right are: (front row) Billy Clingman, Harry Loucks, Howie Camnitz, Gene DeMontreville, Bill O'Hara, Butler, Wilder, and George Blackburn; (back row) Bill Kemmer, George Yeager, Royale Clark, George Morarity, Carlos Smith, Isaac Durrett, manager Mique "Mike" Finn, *The Toledo News-Bee* reporter Richard J. "Dick" Meade, and Watty Lee. DeMontreville wears the uniform of his former Washington team, and Camnitz may be in the uniform of his former Pittsburgh club. Butler and Wilder did not play a game for Toledo in 1905. Dick Meade was with the *News-Bee*, finally as sports editor, until his death in 1935, except from 1926 to 1928, when he was president of the Mud Hens. (Marc Okkonen.)

William Armour came to Toledo as owner of the Mud Hens beginning in 1907, having been here before, as an outfielder for the 1892 Toledo Black Pirates. Armour began the 1907 season not only as owner, but also as president and field manager. He was so successful in his first two seasons that the Mud Hens outgrew downtown Armory Park. His efforts led to the construction of Swayne Field, which opened on July 3, 1909. The capital for the venture was purported to be his, but he may have been the front man for Cleveland's Charlie Somers. Armour gave up managing after two seasons, but headed the business through the 1911 season. Before coming to Toledo, he had managed five seasons in Cleveland and Detroit, and it was in Detroit that he made one of baseball's greatest deals when he got Ty Cobb to sign for $700 and a $200 per month salary. (Toledo Lucas-County Public Library.)

This penny postcard photograph depicts the 1907 Mud Hens, William Armour's first Toledo club. This team finished in a strong second place, just two games behind the Columbus Senators. From left to right are: (front row) John Sutthoff, Homer Smoot, Master Clarke, Josh Clarke, William Clarke, and George Perring; (middle row) Harry Armbruster, Harry Eells, president and manager William Armour, Clyde Williams, and Fred Abbott; (back row) Jap Barbeau, Edward Pokorney, Grover Gillen, Hi West, Bill Lattimore, Charles Chech, Stephen Reagan, and Grover Land. Chech led the pitching staff with 25 wins, setting the league record with 14 strikeouts in a game and winning a doubleheader in the process. Outfielders Armbruster (.322) and Joshua Clarke (.321) were the leading hitters. (Friend of the author.)

The 1907 Mud Hens were good enough and popular enough to have several of their members featured on tobacco cards. Pitcher Bill Lattimore was a Mud Hen for just one season; Harry Hinchman played only two games at second base in 1907, but became a fixture there for the next five seasons; and Fred Abbott was the team's first-line catcher for five years from 1906 through 1910. (Library of Congress, Prints and Photographs Division.)

Swayne Field's opening ceremonies included a flag raising at the centerfield flagpole. The flagpole was in play, but it was a long way—the distance to the fence in center field was 482 feet. The outfield fence, seen here, was the first in America to be constructed of concrete. The left field portion still stands. (Friend of the author.)

When Swayne Field opened its gates in 1909, it was as fine a ball park as there was in America. Born of necessity, as its predecessor Armory Park seated too few, the new park was the brainchild of Noah Swayne and Bill Armour. Swayne, a long time team board member, purchased the land and leased it to the club. Armour, the team's president and front man for Cleveland's Charlie Somers, supplied the capital. Construction at Monroe Street and Detroit Avenue began on March 6, and was completed in time for the first game on July 3, 1909. Previous parks had been built of wood and were firetraps. Swayne Field was one of the country's first to be constructed of concrete and steel, the same year as the major leagues' first such park, Philadelphia's Shibe. The first game in Swayne Field was a memorable one, with the Mud Hens losing to arch rival Columbus 11–12 in 18 innings while 9,350 looked on. (Friend of the author.)

CHARLEY HICKMAN'S HOME RUN. ·8-B-2·
OPENING DAY AT SWAYNE FIELD TOLEDO. O. JULY 3ʳ 09.

The opening of Swayne Field was a major event in Toledo in the summer of 1909, and was commemorated by a series of penny postcards. This card depicts the first home run at the new park, by Mud Hen outfielder Charlie "Piano Legs" Hickman. Swayne Field had a huge playing area, and was not designed with over-the-fence home runs in mind. Nevertheless, Hickman, a powerful hitter and veteran of 12 major league seasons, hit one the opposite way and onto Detroit Avenue beyond the fence. (Friend of the author.)

This tobacco card, probably issued in 1911, features two of Toledo's Mud Hens. The front of the card depicts Charlie Hickman at bat in front of the fence described above. Harry Hinchman, second baseman, is shown on the reverse, also at Swayne Field. The batting and fielding statistics for both are also shown on the back side. Both players were mainstays in the Toledo lineup, Hickman from 1908–1911 and Hinchman from 1907–1912. (Library of Congress, Prints and Photographs Division.)

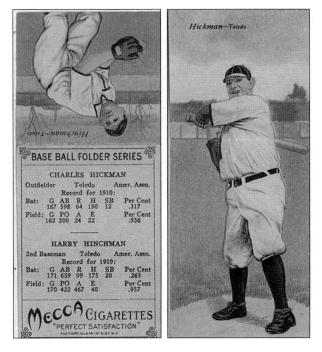

The 1912 Toledo Mud Hens was a good team, perhaps the strongest Toledo had produced to that point, and certainly the best since the club became affiliated with the American Association in 1902. They won 98 games and finished in second place under the leadership of manager Topsy Harsell. Cy Falkenberg was the team's top pitcher with a 25–8 record, while 21-year-old shortstop Ray Chapman (not in this picture) was the leading hitter. Chapman was destined to become the only player killed on a major league ball field. Chapman died in 1920 after being struck in the head with a pitched ball. The pitcher, Carl Mays, would later become a Mud Hen as well. Pictured from left to right are: (front row) Lefty George, Harry Niles, Earle Gardner, secretary George B. Wild, manager Topsy Harsell, Frederick Derrick, Grover Land, and Bunk Congalton; (middle row) unnamed mascot, Brodenhagen, Jim Riley, Mike McCormick, Larry Kopf, Otto Burns, and Walter Walsh; (back row) Harry Krause, Allan Collamore, Bill James, Cy Falkenberg, William James, and Herman Bronkie. (National Baseball Hall of Fame and Library, Cooperstown, N.Y.)

This 1913 Toledo Mud Hens team photograph is similar to those of the previous two years as the players appear in street clothes, but rather than in a studio they pose at Swayne Field. In keeping with the fashion of the times, all wear a hat. Pictured from left to right are: (front row) Otto Burns, Jay Kirke, Jim Baskette, Charlie Jones, Jim Baskette, secretary George B. Wild, manager Herman Bronkie, Bill Stumpf, Red Bluhm, Cal Crum, and Billy Southworth; (back row) Elmer Smith, Rex DeVogt, Lee Dashner, Earle Gardner, Allan Collamore, Oscar Zesing, Raymond Williams, Henry Benn, George Young, Clarence Teague, Johnny Bassler, and unidentified. The season was one of futility for the Hens who finished tied for seventh place, just one game out of the American Association cellar. Individual futility was experienced by pitcher Jim Baskette, who lost a no-hit game 0–1 at Minneapolis on July 13. Many of these players moved to Cleveland as the franchise was shifted there for the next two years. (National Baseball Hall of Fame and Library, Cooperstown, N.Y.)

33

—TOLEDO SOUTH-MICHIGAN LEAGUE BASEBALL CLUB- 1914—

—CLASS C LEAGUE—

Toledo lost the Mud Hens for two seasons beginning in 1914. Charlie Somers of Cleveland owned both the Mud Hens and the Cleveland American League club. In order to keep the expansion Federal League out of Cleveland, Somers moved the Mud Hens to Cleveland. Schedules were arranged so that a Somers team was always at home in Cleveland. The plan did keep the Federal League out of Cleveland, but Toledo lost its team in the process. The Toledo void was filled by a Class C minor league team that was entered in the Southern Michigan Association. The Toledo contingent was known as the Soumichers and sometimes referred to as the little Mud Hens. The league season was divided into halves with Toledo finishing third among the ten teams for the first half. However, attendance was so poor at Swayne Field that Toledo played all of its games on the road for the second half of the season. Toledo played horribly and finished dead last while winning only nine of 67 games. The debacle of 1914 was not repeated the next season, and Toledo was without baseball. The Federal League collapsed after two seasons, and the American Association team was returned to Toledo by Roger Bresnahan for the 1916 season. Only a portion of the 50 players used by the club throughout the course of the season are shown here. From left to right are unidentified, Ted Turner, John Cosma, Benny Seiger, Hugh Sweeney, captain Chuck Nichols, James Baxter, Walter Hart, Frank Burke, Bert Dennis, William Rodgers, John Pendry, and player and manager Topsy Hartsell. Hartsell was a veteran player of ten major league seasons and had managed the Mud Hens in 1912 and 1913. (Ralph Lin Weber.)

34

The 1917 Toledo Iron Men are seen here with some friends and members of the Toledo press at spring training camp at Dawson Springs, Kentucky. From left to right are: (first row) Steve Evans, Abe Bowman, president, manager and player Roger Bresnahan with dog, Colonel Hamby, John Fluhrer, Bunny Fabrique, and Charles Donnelly; (second row) Al Schultz, Lute Boone, Charlie Mullen, Hugh Bedient, Dazzy Vance, and Neal Brady; (third row) Mayor of Dawson Springs Ed Sweeney, Russ Ford, Roy Hartzell, *The Toledo News-Bee* reporter Mitch Woodbury, and the president of the Dawson Springs Chamber of Commerce; (back row) Angel Aragon, Bill Bailey, Harold Wise, Ray Keating, and *Toledo Times* reporter Harold McNaughton. After purchasing the club, Bresnahan called his team Iron Men for three seasons before reverting to the traditional Mud Hens. Reportedly, he had considered using the name "Bresnahens." (Photo reprinted with permission of *The Toledo Blade*.)

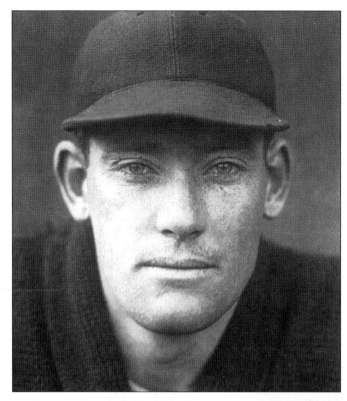

Bill Lamar hit for a .360 batting average over five seasons in Toledo, topped by his .391 in 1923 when he was the American Association's batting champion. Lamar, a Mud Hen in 1918 and again from 1921 through 1924, has been named to the Toledo All-Twentieth-Century Team as an outfielder, and played nine seasons in the major leagues. (Robert Koehler.)

Jim Thorpe was named the greatest all-around athlete of the first half of the twentieth century by the Associated Press. During 1921, his only season as a Mud Hen, he demonstrated why. Showing a blend of speed and power, he batted .353, stole 39 bases, and drove in 112 runs. This season was Thorpe's finest in a 12-year professional baseball career that included six seasons in the National League. On July 13, the clean-up hitting center fielder equaled the American Association record with three home runs in leading the Hens to a 17–4 win over the Brewers in Milwaukee. Most remembered for his gold medal performances in the pentathlon and decathlon in the 1912 Olympics, Thorpe was twice All-American in football and played both football and baseball professionally. He was the first president of America's first professional football league and held a franchise along with Mud Hens owner Roger Bresnahan. (Photo reprinted with permission of *The Toledo Blade*.)

Three members of the 1922 Toledo Mud Hens were future Hall of Famers; however, the team still managed to lose 101 games, finishing one game ahead of last place Columbus in the American Association. Bound for the Hall were 16-year-old third baseman Freddie Lindstrom, pitcher and first baseman Bill Terry, and president, coach, and part-time manager Roger Bresnahan. Pictured from left to right are: (front row) Lee King, Bill Lamar, Bill Terry, manager and player Possum Whitted, Bill Black, Paul McCullough, Ed Konetchy, and secretary Bill Wicks; (middle row) Doc Ayers, Freddie Lindstrom, Bob Wright, James Murphy, Alan Hill, and Hugh Bedient; (back row) Al Wickland, Joe Giard, Brad Kocher, Roy Grimes, and Frank Murphy. (The Toledo Mud Hens.)

Noah Swayne, shown here extending greetings from his private box at Swayne Field, was instrumental in the 1909 building of the ball park that bore his name. Local legend is that Swayne donated the property at the corner of Monroe Street and Detroit Avenue to the club. He did provide the land, but not without remuneration. According to records maintained by Lucas County (Ohio) Recorders Office, he leased the property to the Toledo Exhibition Company and did not relinquish his interest until just days before his death in 1922. In addition to annual payments of $1,902.00, the lease provided that Swayne receive "the exclusive use of…a box of sufficient floor space to accommodate six chairs comfortably…and …tickets or passes not to exceed six in number." Swayne Field was his brainchild, and it had a long life, spanning 46 seasons of professional baseball. The park was Toledo's outdoor sports center as amateur baseball, football, Negro league baseball, and major league exhibitions were played there. When reporting the death of Swayne, *The Toledo Blade* said, "Probably no man in Toledo in the last 50 years was more closely identified with the social, political, religious, and financial life of the city…." He died a millionaire and Swayne Field was his legacy. He is buried in Toledo's historic Woodlawn Cemetery. (Photo reprinted with permission of *The Toledo Blade*.)

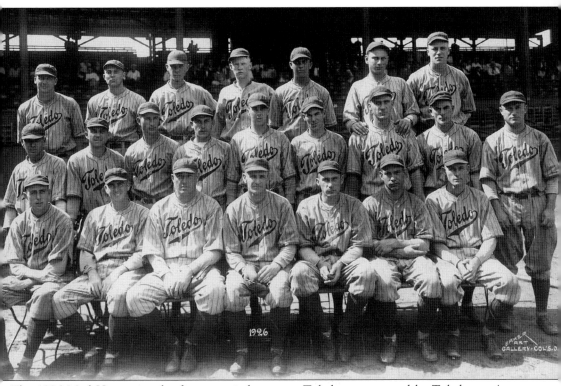

The 1926 Mud Hens were the first twentieth-century Toledo team owned by Toledoans. A group of local investors formed the Toledo Holding Company in a deal put together by Toledo attorneys John McMahon and Oscar Smith; both would be involved with the club for a number of years. The group also gained control of Swayne Field from New York interests and hired Dick Meade, the long time Sports Editor of *The Toledo News-Bee,* as president. Casey Stengel had been hired by the previous owner, Joseph O'Brien, to manage the club, and so was already on board. Stengel was involved with the Worcester, Massachusetts club as president, manager, and player the previous season, but made himself available by some cunning. According to Robert Creamer in *Stengel: His Life and Times,* Stengel "...released himself as a player. He then fired himself as manager and resigned as president, and O'Brien formally engaged him as manager of Toledo." Stengel quickly assembled a team of veterans that produced Toledo's first winning season in five years. Pictured from left to right are: (front row) Freddie Maguire, Tim McNamara, Jeff Pfeffer, manager Casey Stengel, Roy Grimes, Johnnie Heving, and Ernie Maun; (middle row) Pete Cote, Heine Groh, Bevo LeBourveau, Ibert Hermann, Ernest Woolfolk, Woody English, Ray Grimes, Bobby Veach, and Luke Urban; (back row) Pip Koehler, Robert Caffrey, Wilbur Cooper, Milton Phillips, Benny Frey, Paul McCullough, and Rosy Ryan. (The Toledo Mud Hens.)

Opposite: Babe Ruth is shown here with Frank Patrick Gilhooley, Sr. holding his son, Frank, Jr. The elder Gilhooley, a Toledoan, played nine seasons of major league baseball with the Cardinals, Yankees, and Red Sox and followed that with an outstanding ten-year career in the International League. He and Ruth were teammates with the Boston Red Sox in 1919. During that season Ruth played both the outfield and pitched for the Red Sox. When he pitched, Gilhooley filled his outfield position. The younger Frank began broadcasting Toledo baseball games in 1953, and will still be in the booth for the Mud Hens 2003 season. (Courtesy Frank Patrick Gilhooley, Jr.)

The Toledo Mud Hens of 1927 was the best team in all minor league baseball and the finest that the city has ever produced. Under the tutelage of manager Casey Stengel, the Hens won their first American Association pennant and went on to defeat a powerful and favored Buffalo club in the Junior World Series. Stengel had built a club of major league veterans sprinkled with a few youngsters that won the last ten games of the season, all on the road, and swiped the league title by winning a doubleheader on the season's last day. Pictured from left to right are: (front row) Pete Cote, Jesse Barnes, George Milstead, Roy Grimes, Mickey O'Neil, Joe Bush, and Everett Scott; (middle row) Pip Koehler, Paul McCullough, Freddie Maguire, Emilio Palmero, Roy Parmalee, manager Casey Stengel, Joe Kelly, Jeff Pfeffer, and Rosy Ryan; (back row) Edward Sullivan, Charles Nalbock, Bobby Veach, Walt Huntzinger, Jack Wisner, William Marriott, Ernie Maun, Johnnie Heving, and Byron Speece. (Toledo-Lucas County Public Library, Ralph Lin Weber collection.)

Bobby Veach came to Toledo following a 14-year major league career, mostly with the Detroit Tigers where he played alongside Hall of Fame outfielders Ty Cobb, Sam Crawford, and Harry Heilmann. While at Toledo from 1926 through 1930, he batted .356, won an American Association batting title, and was a member of Toledo's only Junior World Series champion team; he has also been named to the Toledo All-Twentieth-Century Team. (Robert Koehler.)

Over his six seasons at the Toledo helm, Casey Stengel occasionally put himself in the lineup. On June 22, during the 1927 pennant drive, Stengel inserted himself as a pinch-hitter in the bottom of the eleventh inning at Swayne Field and, with two outs and a full count, delivered a two-run home run to win the game 10–9. (Robert Koehler.)

Babe Ruth is shown here at Toledo's Swayne Field in 1928. Ruth first appeared in Toledo with the Yankees on September 15, 1920, in the first of two exhibition appearances he would make in Toledo with New York. The Babe pleased onlookers with two home runs, one a grand slam, and drove in six runs. Despite his efforts, the Mud Hens prevailed 8–7 in ten innings. Ruth returned on September 13, 1928, with baseball's reigning World Series champion New York Yankees to play the reigning Junior World Series champion Toledo Mud Hens. The Yankee appearance was partial compensation for pitcher Rosy Ryan who had been dealt to them by Toledo manager Casey Stengel the previous year. Ruth played first base and hit a home run onto Detroit Avenue. The regular Yankee first baseman, Lou Gehrig, played in the outfield and also had a home run in the 8–6 Yankee victory. Oddly, Ryan was the winning pitcher for the New Yorkers. Ruth also appeared at Swayne Field as a pitcher for the Boston Red Sox in 1917. (Photo reprinted with permission of *The Toledo Blade*.)

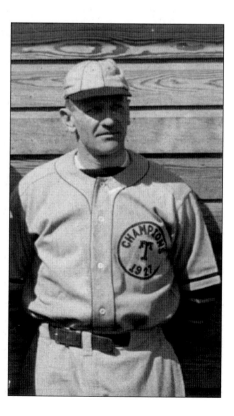

Casey Stengel's Junior World Series Championship of 1927 earned the Mud Hens this special uniform insignia for the following year. Toledo did not come close to repeating as they dropped all the way to sixth place in the American Association. Their wins dropped from 101 to 79, and the season record attendance of 316,328 in 1927 dipped to 182,814. (Photo reprinted with permission of *The Toledo Blade*.)

This preseason photograph of the 1929 Mud Hens was taken at Swayne Field. In the background, behind the left field wall, is the ever present Toledo Edison coal pile. Hopes were high that this team, with many of the same players, would repeat the 1927 championship. Instead, the Mud Hens finished last in the American Association, and suffered the first of Casey Stengel's pair of 100-loss seasons. Pictured from left to right are: (up front) announcer and mascot Ducky Walinski; (bottom row) Roy Parmalee, David Klinger, John Tate, Herb Thomas, Jones, William Raab, James Sweeny, and Ed Taylor; (middle row) Walt Huntzinger, Emilio Palmero, Pip Koehler, manager Casey Stengel, Harry McCurdy, Edward Moore, Jack Warner, Johnny Neun, and Bobby Veach; (top row) Garland Buckeye, Beale, Ernie Wingard, Ray Lucas, Jeff Pfeffer, Tim McNamara, Powers, Jimmy Ring, Eddie Brown, and Howard Freigau. (Photo reprinted with permission of *The Toledo Blade*.)

The 1929 Toledo Mud Hens prepare to take early season batting practice at Swayne Field. This view from the stands behind home plate looks toward Detroit Avenue and shows the centerfield bleachers. The short man near the front is Ducky Walinski, the team's batboy, field announcer, and mascot for six seasons (1925–1930). (Photo reprinted with permission of *The Toledo Blade*.)

Carl "Ducky" Walinski is shown here announcing to the crowd at Swayne Field on opening day in 1929. Walinski was hired by Mud Hens secretary Jim McGraw (brother of New York Giants manager John McGraw) at the age of 15 in 1925. Ducky's duties—for which he was paid 25 cents per day—included caring for uniforms, cleaning the clubhouse, running errands for players, and cleaning shoes, as well as looking after equipment during practice sessions and games. Walinski later earned local fame traveling the city as a rolling advertisement for Buckeye Beer. He would roam Toledo streets on roller skates, sometimes in the company of a goat, plugging his product at taverns along the way. He became known as Bucky then. (Photo reprinted with permission of *The Toledo Blade*.)

Bevo LeBourveau compiled the highest career batting average, .380, of any Toledo player. The popular outfielder was a Mud Hen for four seasons (1926, 1927, 1930, 1931), compiling batting averages of .377, .346, .380, and .446 (88 games), respectively. While at Toledo, he won two American Association batting titles and was a member of Toledo's only Junior World Series champion team. He has been named to the Toledo All-Twentieth-Century Team. LeBouroveau also owns the American Association career batting record, compiling a .360 average over ten seasons with Toledo, Milwaukee, Kansas City, and Columbus. He played four seasons for Philadelphia of the National League early in his 16-year career, but never made it back to the majors despite his gaudy batting statistics. Bevo LeBourveau was sold to Columbus during the 1931 season when the Toledo team was on the verge of financial collapse. (Robert Koehler.)

Pip Koehler was a fixture in Casey Stengel's Toledo lineup for the six seasons (1926–1931) that they were together at Toledo. Not spectacular, but very good and always steady, Koehler was a versatile and outstanding defensive player who batted .275 over his Toledo career. He hit .364 in Toledo's only Junior World Series appearance as the Mud Hens won against the Buffalo Bisons in 1927. Koehler played 886 games for the Mud Hens (second only to Bobby Gilks' all-time record of 1,040) in the outfield, at third base, and shortstop.

Concurrent with his baseball career, Koehler played 11 seasons of professional basketball, some at the major level with the Fort Wayne Chiefs of the National Basketball Association's forerunner American League. (Photos reprinted with permission of *The Toledo Blade*.)

Casey Stengel, one of baseball's most colorful figures, is shown here at the Mud Hens spring training camp at Miami Beach, Florida, on March 22, 1931. Pictured with Stengel is Kelly Herbst, captain of the House of David team that had just lost to Toledo 6–5. Stengel managed the Toledo Mud Hens from 1926 through 1931. His 1927 team was Toledo's best ever, winning the Junior World Series over Buffalo. (Author's collection.)

Roger Bresnahan, on the left, and Casey Stengel together at Swayne Field in 1929 in a photograph dated by Stengel's distinctive cap. Toledoan Bresnahan had done it all in baseball. He had been a major league player, coach, and manager. At Toledo, he owned the team for seven seasons, from 1917 through 1923. During that time he was club president, and sometimes managed, coached, and played. He had begun his professional career as a 19-year-old pitcher with the Mud Hens in 1898. Stengel had assembled Toledo's greatest team in 1927, but would suffer the first of his two 100-loss seasons at Toledo in 1929. Both were headed for the Hall of Fame. (Photo reprinted with permission of *The Toledo Blade*.)

Steve O'Neill was the Toledo Mud Hens coach in 1933, manager in 1934 and 1935, and part-time catcher for all three of those years. In 1935, he batted .313 as a 42 year old. One of four brothers to make it to the major leagues, he caught 17 major league seasons, mostly for Cleveland. (Photo reprinted with permission of *The Toledo Blade*.)

Mud Hens pitcher Dizzy Trout and veteran Toledo outfielder Mike Powers greet their fans and sign autographs in 1937 at one of the five Blade-Mud Hens Roosts. Trout was about to move on to Detroit and a championship major league career while Powers was winding down a stellar Toledo career. In six Mud Hen seasons the all-star Powers hit a robust .334 and had a consecutive game hitting streak of 32 in 1935, falling just one shy of Bevo LeBourveau's mark set in 1926 into 1927. (Photo reprinted with permission of *The Toledo Blade*.)

These unidentified 1934 Mud Hen hopefuls gathered at Toledo's Union Station on March 15, 1934, to travel to their spring training site at Orange, Texas. By the time the season ended on September 16, the Hens had won just 68 of 153 American Association games to finish in sixth place, just ahead of St. Paul and Kansas City. Minneapolis won the pennant that season and was followed in the standings by Columbus, Milwaukee, Louisville, and Indianapolis. (Photo reprinted with permission of *The Toledo Blade*.)

Flea Clifton, Toledo third baseman, slides safely home in the first inning of the April 25, 1937, game against Louisville at Swayne Field. The Colonels' catcher Ray Berres turns to retrieve the ball which had been thrown high over his head. The Hens went on to win 11–0 behind the three hit pitching of Slick Coffman. (Photo reprinted with permission of *The Toledo Blade.*)

This 1937 Toledo Mud Hens scorecard was sold at Swayne Field for a nickel. It featured action photos on the cover and contained advertisements, both local and national, throughout. There is a house ad on the cover, "be comfortable—rent a soft, clean cushion." Rentals were ten cents. Current lineup sheets were pasted inside for scoring the game. Ticket prices for 1937 were listed: Boxes $1.00, Grandstand 75¢, Ladies Grand 50¢, Pavilion 50¢, and Child's pavilion 50 cents, tax included. (Arnold Bunge, Jr. collection.)

These 1937 Mud Hens had just completed the season with seven straight wins and would tie for the American Association pennant with Columbus if the Red Birds lost later in the day. But Columbus did not lose, and the Hens finished a close second. The fine performance earned the Mud Hens their first berth in the American Association playoffs, but they dropped the first set to the Milwaukee Brewers four games to two. Babe Herman, Alta Cohen, and Ed Coleman are seated in the foreground, while standing from left to right are Chet Morgan, manager Fred Haney, Jimmy Adair, Frank Croucher, Clyde Hatter (behind the catcher's mitt), and Mike Powers. (Photo reprinted with permission of *The Toledo Blade*.)

Ralph Winegarner had 11 pitching wins and 11 home runs with a .345 batting average for the Mud Hens in 1932, filling the unusual role of pitcher and pinch-hitter. His versatility was a big plus for manager Bibb Falk. He was a journeyman ball player who played four years, in two stops, in Toledo among his 16 in professional baseball. He spent six seasons in the major leagues. During his time in Toledo, he alternated between the mound, third base, first base, the outfield, and pinch-hitting. (Photo reprinted with permission of *The Toledo Blade*.)

Opposite: This is a small part of an August 15, 1937 Sunday doubleheader crowd that was so large that some fans were seated behind ropes in the outfield at Swayne Field. The 1937 season was the most successful for Toledo baseball since the pennant-winning year of 1927 in terms of both team performance and fan attendance. More fans—259,267—came to watch than in any other year in Toledo history, except for that 1927 year when 316,328 streamed through the Swayne Field turnstiles. The 12,185 there that day had hoped to see the Mud Hens move into first place in the American Association, but the locals dropped both games to the Columbus Red Birds. At the end of the day, Minneapolis was in first place with a 71–50 record, followed by Columbus 69–52, and Toledo 68–53. The three teams battled the rest of the way, with Columbus winning the pennant by one game over Toledo, and Minneapolis two back of the Hens. (Photo reprinted with permission of *The Toledo Blade*.)

The 1938 Toledo Mud Hens squad arrives at Toledo after completing its spring training and exhibition schedule through the south. Pictured from left to right are: (front row) Benny McCoy, Buddy Hancken, Dizzy Trout, Stan Corbett, Pat McLaughlin, Roy House, and Johnny Johnson; (back row) Emmett Nelson, Chet Morgan, coach Myles Thomas, Johnny Zapor, Cecil Dunn, Oliver Thomas, Bob Harris, Joe Roxbury, manager Fred Haney, Joe Greenberg, Charlie Gelbert, Ed Coleman, Vic Sorrell, vice-president Jim Cobley, George Archie, president Waldo Shank, and trainer Andy Perna. (Photo reprinted with permission of *The Toledo Blade*.)

The 1938 Toledo Mud Hens pose at Swayne Field with the scoreboard and the Toledo Edison steam plant in the background. The team finished fifth in the American Association that season. Pictured from left to right are: (front row) trainer Doc Perna, Joe Rogalski, Chet Wilburn, Chet Laabs, and batboy Frank Gilhooley; (middle row) Bob Linton, Bob Harris, Roy Cullenbine, manager Fred Haney, Johnny Johnson, Benny McCoy, Buddy Hancken, and Charles Treadway; (back row) Charlie Gelbert, Ed Coleman, Al Benton, Firpo Marberry, Emmett Nelson, George Archie, Fred Johnson, Gordie Hinkle, and coach Myles Thomas. Batboy Gilhooley continues with the Mud Hens in 2003 as radio broadcaster. (National Baseball Hall of Fame and Library, Cooperstown, N.Y.)

This unusual action shot of April 21, 1940 was alertly taken by *The Toledo Blade*'s Tom O'Reilly and published in that newspaper the next day. "In the seventh inning of yesterday's Toledo-Milwaukee game at Swayne Field, catcher Hal Spindel beat out a slow roller to third base, and is seen sliding desperately into first base to win the decision. Pitcher Bob Kline fielded the ball and slipped as he threw. He collapsed an instant later from the wrench to his anatomy and had to be carried from the field." Spindel was the Mud Hens regular catcher for three seasons (1940–1942). (Rex Hamann.)

Golfing legend Byron Nelson was head professional at Toledo's Inverness Club when he appeared in a 1942 exhibition game for Toledo. Shown here in catcher's gear with Mud Hen manager Fred Haney, Nelson actually played the outfield in a Swayne Field contest with the Hens' parent St. Louis Browns. Haney managed the Mud Hens for six seasons, four of them as a player and manager, and ranks among Toledo's best all-time managers. His ten years managing in the major leagues included back-to-back pennants and a World Series championship at Milwaukee. (Temple University Libraries.)

Waldo Shank, shown here with Mud Hens manager Zack Taylor at the start of the 1941 season, was president of the Toledo club for nine years. He had headed a group of local investors that took the club out of receivership in 1933, saving baseball for Toledo. Shank's teams finished in the second division every year except for 1937, when the Mud Hens finished in second place, just one game behind Columbus. He sold the club to the St. Louis Browns in 1942, and claimed to have lost money every year except for the successful 1937 campaign. Taylor was a 16-year major league catcher who managed in Toledo in 1940 and part of 1941 and later managed the St. Louis Browns for five seasons. (Photo reprinted with permission of *The Toledo Blade*.)

The 1943 edition of the Toledo Mud Hens, shown here at Swayne Field, won exactly as often as they lost, finished fourth in the American Association, and qualified for the league playoffs. Pictured from left to right are: (front row) Floyd Baker, Bill Seinsoth, Jack Kramer, Red Hayworth, manager Jack Fournier, Len Schulte, Jim Bucher, Nick Gregory, Hal Epps, and Phil Weintruab, with mascot Rusty Gilliand up front; (back row) trainer Doc Perna, Tony Criscola, Dick Kimble, Fred Sanford, Ardys Keller, Loy Hanning, John Whitehead, Bill Cox, Sid Peterson, Bob Boken, Bob Wren, and Lin Storti. Season highlights included a no-hit game by Jack Kramer at Louisville on September 11 and utility man Bob Boken's perfect day at bat, six hits in six tries on May 12. (Toledo-Lucas County Public Library, Ralph Lin Weber collection.)

Eddie Ignasiak, a product of the Toledo sandlots, was a journeyman minor league player who played in nine different leagues in a 13-year professional career. He grew up in the shadow of Swayne Field, attending St. Stanislaus and Robinson Junior High schools, and later returned to play at Swayne with the Mud Hens of 1944 and 1945. He was a switch-hitting first baseman and possessed such defensive skill that he was named to his league's all-star team six times during his career. His Mud Hen teammate Bobby Wren called him "the slickest fielder I ever saw." Ignasiak was an extremely popular player in Toledo and was welcomed home in 1944 with "Eddie Ignasiak Day" at Swayne Field. Eddie was honored that day, but the Mud Hens were humbled, losing in record fashion to the Milwaukee Brewers 28–0. Later, as a successful Toledo business proprietor, Ignasiak quipped, "I only had one weakness as a professional ball player, and that was the pitched ball." (Toledo-Lucas County Public Library, Ralph Lin Weber collection.)

The higher classifications of baseball's minor leagues continued to play a full schedule during World War II, as did the major leagues. This was unlike the World War I experience when many leagues suspended play, and others like Toledo's American Association greatly reduced the length of the season in 1918. The 1944 program shown here features Uncle Sam on the front cover, Lady Liberty on the back cover, and patriotic slogans and pleas from advertisers throughout to buy war bonds. Toledo baseball historian Ralph Lin Weber published *The Toledo Baseball Guide of the Mud Hens* during the war. The book contained the slogan "Toledo prefers baseballs to cannon balls" as well as a listing of Mud Hen players who enlisted in the armed services, ten in both 1942 and 1943, and another four in 1944. (Arnold Bunge, Jr. collection.)

TOLEDO 1944
MUD HENS
OFFICIAL BASEBALL MAGAZINE   Price 10¢

GENE RICHARD
TOLEDO'S FASTEST RECAP SERVICE
1222 MADISON AT 13TH ST.
PHONE ADAMS 5114

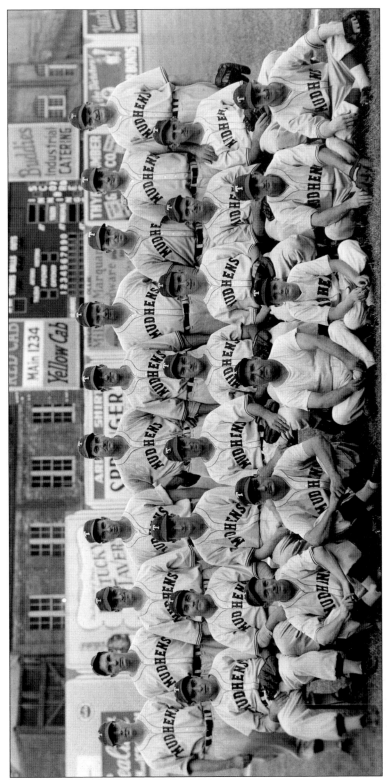

The 1944 Toledo Mud Hens won 95 games and finished in second place in the American Association, seven games back of the Milwaukee Brewers. Their success was helped by the heroics of the popular outfielder and catcher Boris "Babe" Martin who hit a solid .350 and was named the league's most valuable player by its sportswriters. Bill Seinsoth led the pitching staff in innings pitched and wins with 16. Walter Brown won a 1–0 no-hit game at Milwaukee in August. Pictured from left to right are: (front row) Don Smith, George Corona, trainer Doc Perna, mascot Rusty Gilliand, Dick Kimble, and Len Schulte; (middle row) Al LaMacchia, Earl Jones, Stretch Goedde, manager Ollie Marquardt, Bill Burgo, Cliff Fannin, Fred Reinhart, and Harry Kimberlin; (back row) Bob Wren, Bill Sullivan, Walter Brown, Ox Miller, Bill Seinsoth, Ed Ignasiak, John Whitehead, Joe Schultz, Babe Martin, and Bob Boken. Marquardt, Ignasiak, and catcher Walt Missler (not in picture) were native Toledoans. (Author's collection.)

Some of the 1945 Toledo Mud Hens show the team's new uniforms before the season's inaugural contest with the Louisville Colonels at Swayne Field. Pictured from left to right are Don Smith, Bob Wren, Fred Reinhart, Dick Kimble, Bob Okrie, Bob Boken, Ed Ignasiak, Red Lanfersieck, and Blackie Thompson. Though Toledoan Ignasiak had a pair of doubles, the Hens dropped the opening game 4–2. (Photo reprinted with permission of The Toledo Blade.)

This action shot of a Phil Weintraub grand slam home run is captured from deep in the stands at Swayne Field. Weintraub connected during the second game of a doubleheader against the Milwaukee Brewers on July 11, 1943. The picture was taken by *The Toledo Blade* photographer Dave West, who had his camera with him as he was seated in the grandstand. The veteran Weintraub was the American Association's top fielding first baseman in 1942 and led the Hens with 16 home runs and 96 runs batted in while hitting for a 334 average. (Toledo-Lucas County Public Library, Ralph Lin Weber collection.)

This aerial view of Swayne Field was taken sometime after 1944. The vertical roadway is Detroit Avenue which intersects Monroe Street at the southeast corner of the park. The curved inner fence was added for the 1945 season so that Swayne Field could conform to the home run style of play that had become popular since the park was built. Swayne Field was the center for outdoor sports in Toledo. Besides being home for the American Association Mud Hens and Sox, it also hosted three Negro league teams, baseball exhibitions featuring black and major league teams, and amateur baseball. Swayne Field was also the scene of occasional football games, rodeos, prize fights, foot races, dog races, automobile daredevil shows, and even beauty pageants. (Toledo-Lucas County Public Library.)

Jerry Witte set the Toledo single season home record with 46 in 1946, his first season back in baseball after serving three years in World War II. The Hens first baseman added three more that year in the American Association All-Star game and another two when he was called up to the St. Louis Browns late in the season. Since Swayne Field was built in 1909, home run hitters faced a left field wall that was 379 feet away. The right handed hitting Witte took advantage of that distance being shortened to 330 feet in 1945. Witte was a journeyman minor league player who could hit home runs anywhere. He had 308 in a 13-year minor league career topped by a season high of 50 with Dallas of the Texas League in 1950. Jerry Witte has held the Toledo record longer than any other player as shown by the following evolution of the record: two by Sam Barkley in 1883; three by Tony Mullane in 1884; four by Benjamin Drischell in 1888; six by Perry Werden in 1890; 16 by Ed McFarland in 1894; 24 by Erve Beck in 1930 and again by Ernie Wingard in 1930; 33 by Hal Trosky in 1933; and finally 46 by Witte in 1946. Witte has held the record for 56 years and was challenged seriously only once, when Phil Hiatt slammed 42 in 1996. (Photo reprinted with permission of *The Toledo Blade*.)

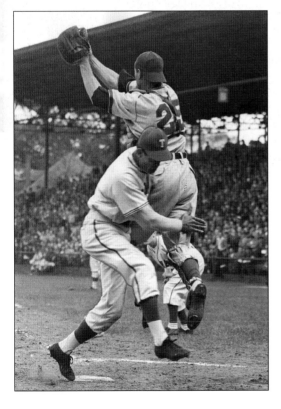

Shown here moving Milwaukee's catcher Marv Felderman off the plate, Jerry Witte scores one of his team-leading 99 runs in 1946. Witte had quite a day in the Hens' Sunday, May 12 doubleheader sweep of the Brewers. He had five hits, including three home runs, before 8,306 at Swayne Field. (Photo reprinted with permission of *The Toledo Blade*.)

George Corona was a Mud Hen for seven seasons (1943–1949). His two best were the war years of 1944 and 1945 when he played regularly in the outfield and hit .308 and .313. He is the last Mud Hen to play as many as seven seasons. Since Corona's time several have played as many as six: Bob Reed, Tom Timmerman, Wayne Comer, and Shawn Hare. (Photo reprinted with permission of *The Toledo Blade*.)

Pete Gray, shown here at Toledo's Swayne Field, was the only one-armed player in major league history. Gray was an outfielder for the Mud Hens in 1946, batting .250 in 48 games. The high point of his Toledo career came when he collected seven hits in eight tries during a Fourth of July doubleheader in Columbus. Despite losing his dominant right arm in an accident when he was six years old, Gray played an eight-year professional career. His Southern Association Most Valuable Player performance for Memphis in 1944 earned him a promotion to the Toledo's parent club, the St. Louis Browns, for the 1945 season. A Browns teammate and former Mud Hen pitcher Al LaMacchia recalled, "You had to marvel at Pete Gray. He was driven to succeed like few people you have ever seen." (Photo reprinted with permission of *The Toledo Blade*.)

The Toledo Mud Hens gather at their spring training camp in Sanford, Florida, in early March, 1947. This picture appeared in *The Toledo Bee* on March 12 with the following caption, "The Mud Hens, just like all other athletes, get a few words of wisdom as they go through their training paces in their spring training camp. Here manager Frank "Pancho" Snyder is dishing out "the word" while a goodly portion of his squad pays attention. The Hens, with nearly a week's work under their belts, are rapidly rounding into playing condition." (Photo reprinted with permission of *The Toledo Blade*.)

Hall of Fame pitcher Cy Young is seen here as he makes a pitch from Swayne Field's mound. The occasion was the annual Field Day of the Old Timers Baseball Association, August 24, 1947. The then 80 year old was paid a $40 fee to help promote the day's baseball events. During his 22-year major league career, Young both won and lost more games than any other pitcher. (Jim VanOrden.)

Toledo artist Robert Parsil created this, the original, depiction of a Mud Hen in 1948. The likeness would later be known as Mortimer. Though Toledo baseball teams had been known as the Mud Hens as early as 1896, this is the first graphic of the team's namesake. (Reprinted with permission of *The Toledo Blade*.)

Mortimer the Mud Hen was unveiled in 1949 by the new owners of the Toledo Mud Hens, the Detroit Tigers. The Tigers purchased the club from the St. Louis Browns, made improvements to the operation and Swayne Field, and introduced Mortimer. (Arnold Bunge, Jr. Collection.)

The 1950 Mud Hen opening day lineup exits the dugout at Swayne Field. The Mud Hens were the top Detroit Tiger farm club and mimicked the parent club's uniforms with old English "Ts" on the shirt and cap and also had a mud hen on the left sleeve. The players from left to right appear in the opening day batting order and are Emil Restaino, cf; Johnny Bero, ss; Don Lund, rf; George Vico, 1b; Austin Knickerbocker, lf; Bobby Mavis, 3b; Alex DeLaGarza, 2b; Eddie Mordarski, c; and Ken Fremming, p. (Photo reprinted with permission of *The Toledo Blade*.)

Marlin Stuart pitched the only perfect game in Toledo baseball history when he beat the Indianapolis Indians 1–0 on June 27, 1950, at Swayne Field. His effort headlines a list of nine no-hitters thrown by Toledo hurlers. The last was by Jose Lima when he beat the Pawtucket Red Sox 3–0 at Ned Skeldon Stadium on August 17, 1994. On nine other occasions, Toledo pitchers have held the opposition hitless, but the games were not classified as no-hitters because they were less than nine innings or Toledo did not win. Among those was a seven-inning "perfect game" by Joe Niekro on July 16, 1972. (National Baseball Hall of Fame and Library, Cooperstown, N.Y.)

The scoreboard at Swayne Field tells the story of Marlin Stuart's perfect game on June 27, 1950. (Photo reprinted with permission of *The Toledo Blade*.)

Mickey Mantle recalled his then finest day for *The Sporting News*. It came in Toledo, July 31, 1951. Mantle had started the season with the Yankees, but the 19-year-old wonder was sent to Kansas City by Casey Stengel for regular work. That night at Swayne Field he had two home runs, a triple, a double, and a single for the cycle-plus in leading his Blues to a 7–0 win over the Mud Hens. Local sportscaster Frank Gilhooley was at that game and recalls that Mantle was ordered to hit in the ninth inning on a 3–0 count by his manager, George Selkirk. It seems that Selkirk was impressed by the standing ovation the large Toledo crowd gave the visitor, and with the game in hand, wanted to please them. Gilhooley says that Mantle twice stepped out of the batter's box to question his manager's hit sign and was then told verbally to hit away. Mantle responded with a drag bunt single toward first base to complete the cycle. Gilhooley says he was "almost to the bullpen" before the ball got to first base. Mantle was one of many future stars who made their way through Toledo on their way to the major leagues. Ted Williams, Willie Mays, Johnny Bench, and Derek Jeter are among those who made stops in Toledo as Mud Hen opponents. (Reprinted by permission of *The Sporting News*.)

The Sporting News Baseball Questionnaire filled out by Mickey Mantle.

Toledo Mud Hens pitcher Dwain "Lefty" Sloat soaks his blistered feet. Sloat was with Toledo for three seasons (1949–1951) as a reliever and spot starter. He was a good enough hitter that he played a little first base as well, and had a .320 batting average for the three years. (Photo reprinted with permission of *The Toledo Blade*.)

This opening day starting lineup was expected to provide the batting punch for the 1952 Toledo Mud Hens. Pictured from left to right are Nino Escalera, cf; Bobby Kellogg, 2b; Stan Spence, 1b; Babe Barna, rf; Ken Guettler, lf; Willie Williams, ss; and Mike Vukmire, 3b. All were in their first, and what would be their only, season in Toledo. Escalera and Williams were the first black men to appear in Toledo uniform since the Walker brothers did so in 1884. Three days later, Bill Powell became the first black man to pitch for Toledo. Yet a fourth black player, infielder Charlie Harmon, began the 1952 season with The Mud Hens, but was released before making a game appearance. The Detroit Tigers had sold the club to Danny Menendez following the 1951 season and the Mud Hens were operating as an independent in 1952. Menendez attempted to move the club to Charleston, West Virginia in late June, but was forbidden from doing so by court injunction. Menendez avoided that ruling simply by playing Toledo's home games in Charleston. No matter the legal status, baseball was gone from Toledo, once again. (Photo reprinted with permission of The Toledo Blade.)

The 1953 Sox were one of Toledo's greatest teams and, perhaps, its greatest surprise. Toledo had lost baseball in June of 1952 when the Mud Hens bolted to Charleston, West Virginia. There were no prospects for baseball in 1953, but just before the season began, the Boston Braves moved to Milwaukee. That shift, the first in the major leagues in 50 years, displaced Milwaukee's American Association defending champions. The Brewers landed in Toledo and went on to give the city a dream season. The city went from no baseball to the pennant seemingly overnight, and its fans set a season attendance record in the process. The Sox beat the Louisville Colonels in the first round of the playoffs, but lost narrowly to Kansas City in the finals, just missing a chance to represent the American Association in the Junior World Series. Pictured from left to right are: (front row) Gene Conley, Bob Chipman, Dick Hoover, Don Edinger, batboy Tommy Beard, trainer Bob Feron, Charlie Bicknell, Jack Daniels, and Lu Marquez; center: Billy Reed, Dewey Williams, Hank Ertman, Bob Montag, manager George Selkirk, Billy Queen, coach Joe Just, Paul Rambone, and Billy Klaus; (back row) Jack Cerin, Buddy Kerr, Glenn Thompson, Jim Solt, Russ Kerns, George Estock, Walt Dubiel, Murray Wall, Virgil Jester, and Sam Jethroe. Bert Thiel is not shown. (Photo reprinted with permission of *The Toledo Blade*.)

71

These young fans at Swayne Field had it right in 1953, but the Glasox or Glass Sox misnomer still persists. When the Milwaukee Braves brought their top minor league team to Toledo, general manager Red Smith discarded the long standing Mud Hens tradition and announced a contest to choose a new name for the team. Designed to create fan interest, the contest did just that. Smith and his committee of four selected the winning entry from among the 500 different names included in the 7,500 total entries. They chose Glass Sox. Toledo learned of the decision on April Fools' Day. Fred W. Schultz, a Community Traction Company bus driver, was the first of 24 to submit the winning nickname. He won two season passes and the wrath of almost everyone in the Toledo area. The public outcry was tremendous. The team switchboard was flooded with calls of protest, petitions were submitted, and the Toledo City Council passed a resolution begging for reconsideration. Smith would not succumb, saying "to change would be a reflection on the committee." But finally came news of a compromise; the team would be known as the Sox. And it was. (Photo reprinted with permission of *The Toledo Blade*.)

Gene Conley is congratulated by young fans at Swayne Field after running his record to 17–6 by beating Kansas City 4–0 on August 5, 1953. The six foot eight inch Conley had just limited the top Yankee farm club on three singles enabling Toledo's Sox to maintain their two-game lead over the Louisville Colonels. Both Conley and the Sox kept up the pace as Toledo won a rare pennant and Gene Conley finished the season with 23 wins. Conley was the American Association's dominant pitcher as he led the league in earned run average, victories, innings pitched, complete games, shutouts. He also compiled the best won-lost percentage. For his efforts, Conley was named the Minor League Player of the Year, the only Toledo player ever so honored. He was also named a pitcher on Toledo's All-Twentieth-Century Team. A gifted all-around athlete, Conley also played professional basketball. He became the first athlete to earn world championship rings in two sports, as a member of the 1958 Milwaukee Braves and as a center on the Boston Celtics three consecutive years beginning with 1958-9. (Photo reprinted with permission of *The Toledo Blade*.)

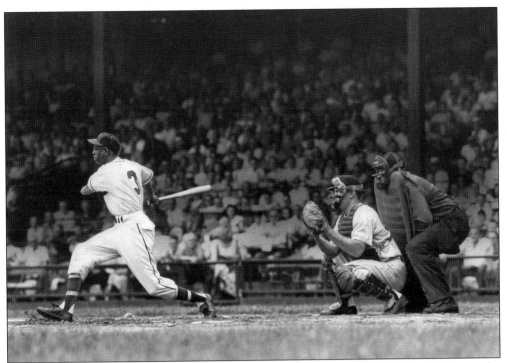

Sam "Jet" Jethroe, a switch hitting and speedy center fielder who sparked Toledo's Sox to the American Association pennant in 1953, is shown here batting left-handed at Toledo's Swayne Field. The team's leading hitter with a .309 batting average, he displayed a blend of speed and power. Jethroe stole 27 bases and scored 137 runs, the most by a twentieth-century Toledo player, and had 32 doubles, 10 triples, and 28 home runs from his lead off spot. (Photo reprinted with permission of *The Toledo Blade*.)

This 1954 sports cartoon appeared in *The Toledo Blade* and recapped the pennant-winning 1953 season of the Toledo Sox. It pointed out that it would be difficult for the 1954 edition to beat the 1953 record. The Blade proved to be correct as the Sox fell to sixth place in the American Association. (Reprinted with permission of *The Toledo Blade*.)

Above: The Toledo Sox brain trust, from left to right, are general manager Red Smith, manager George Selkirk, and coach Joe Just. Selkirk replaced Tommy Holmes just into the 1953 season—otherwise the three were together during the three years the Braves had their top minor league club in Toledo (1953–1955). Smith came to Toledo with the Braves organization, as did Just, a veteran catcher of 15 professional seasons. Selkirk, the man who replaced Babe Ruth in the New York Yankee lineup, had been in the Yankee organization as a player and minor league manager since 1930. He had been let go as the Kansas City manager the previous year because he did not agree with Yankee manager Casey Stengel's shuttling of players between New York and Kansas City. (Photo reprinted with permission of *The Toledo Blade*.)

74

The starting lineup for the 1955 Toledo Sox' season opening game. The opposition was the Denver Bears, managed by Ralph Houk, who were making their American Association debut. Bert Thiel limited the Bears to three singles in a 4–0 win at Swayne Field. Theil aided his cause with his bat by contributing a sacrifice and a pair of doubles. From left to right are Jack Daniels, cf; Vince Garcia, 2b; Pete Whisenant, rf; Lu Marquez, lf; Billy Queen, c; Felix Mantilla, ss; Frank Torre, 1b; Sammy Meeks, 3b; and Bert Thiel, p. (Photo reprinted with permission of *The Toledo Blade*.)

Opposite: Bert Thiel was a member of the Sox pitching staff for all three seasons that the Milwaukee Braves top farm club played in Toledo, 1953 through 1955. In spite of chronic arm problems, he won 27 games, with 16 of those for the sixth place club of 1954. Actually Thiel had five consecutive seasons at the top minor league level of the Braves organization. He was one of those on the American Association pennant-winning teams of 1951 and 1952 in Milwaukee that moved with that franchise to Toledo. This group of players, besides Thiel, was Billy Klaus, Jim Basso, Bob Montag, Billy Reed, Murray Wall, Dick Hoover, and Virgil Jester. They brought a winning attitude to Toledo, and continued their winning ways in notching their third pennant in as many seasons. Thiel, who was somewhat controversial for sometimes "quick pitching" without a windup, continued his 14-year active pitching career through 1961. He stayed in the game as a minor league manager, and major league pitching coach and scout until 1974. While coaching with the Washington Senators, he authored *The Road To Successful Pitching*, a book that stressed the need for sound basic pitching fundamentals. Thiel returned to Toledo's Fifth Third Field in 2002 to help the fans celebrate breaking the attendance record set in 1953 by the fans watching his team at Swayne Field. While there, he stepped to the mound for a ceremonial pitch, and threw yet another strike, nearly half of a century after his first in Toledo. (Photo reprinted with permission of *The Toledo Blade*.)

This June 1955 photograph was taken by Blade photographer Herral Long from the roof of the right field grandstand. No one knew it at the time, but this was the last season that Swayne Field would exist. Just after the season was completed, the parent Milwaukee Braves announced that they were moving their top minor league team to Wichita. The razing of the park began immediately and, a year later, a shopping center stood on the site. Professional baseball would not be played again in northwestern Ohio until 1965. (Photo reprinted with permission of The Toledo Blade.)

76

THREE

The Maumee Era

1965–2001

BASEBALL RETURNED to northwest Ohio in 1965 after an absence of nine seasons, but not to Toledo. Through a community effort led by Ned Skeldon, the Richmond, Virginia franchise was purchased. The Fort Miami Fairgrounds racetrack in Maumee was hurriedly converted into a ballpark by Lucas County. A deal was signed with the New York Yankees to provide players as they agreed to make Toledo home for their top minor league ball club. In a very short time, northwest Ohio had a franchise, a ballpark, and a team. They were called the Toledo Mud Hens of the International League and Maumee, Ohio, was their home.

The Yankee arrangement lasted two seasons, and produced two second division finishes and attendance that was far less than that at Swayne Field a decade earlier. The Tigers and manager Jack Tighe replaced the Yankees for the 1967 season. Though attendance continued to be a disappointment, Tighe turned things around on the field. The 1967 team finished third in the league and won the playoff of the top four finishing clubs to claim the Governor's Cup. This was the first playoff crown won by Toledo since 1897, and is the last. The following season, the Mud Hens won the International League pennant and set a club record for the Maumee Era by winning 83 games. The team won on the strength of its outstanding pitching staff, but it did not repeat as Governor's Cup champion. This team remains the only one of the era to win a flag.

The Tigers continued their working agreement with Toledo for five more seasons. Under five different managers, the Mud Hens had little success either on the field or at the gate. The Philadelphia Phillies and their popular manager Jim Bunning had two losing seasons in 1974 and 1975. Then came the Cleveland Indians for two horrible seasons, both last place finishes.

Three good things happened for the 1978 season. Gene Cook was made general manager, the Minnesota Twins became the major league affiliate, and Cal Ermer became the manager. For his part, Cook promoted the club and also promoted going to baseball games as a family event. He formed a relationship with Jamie Farr and the M*A*S*H television series that sparked the community's interest, and attendance grew steadily during his watch. The Twins brought better players and a capable and stable manager in Ermer, who holds the Toledo all-time managerial records for seasons, games, wins, and losses. Though never spectacular, the Twins' farm club made the playoffs three of nine years.

The Tigers returned for the 1987 season and have remained ever since. On-the-field performance for the remaining years of the era was dismal. Beginning in 1988, the International League adopted a divisional arrangement with four or five clubs in each. In 15 seasons, the Mud Hens finished last ten times, never higher than third place, and never made the playoffs. On the brighter side, attendance continued to grow, and more than tripled under the continued leadership of Gene Cook. In spite of the growth, Toledo ranked near the bottom of the league each year. The growth in fan support, however, was key and the impetus for the effort to build a new park for the Mud Hens, launching a new era in Toledo baseball history.

Year	Team	Finish	W	L	Attendance	League	Manager	Affiliate
1965	Mud Hens	7 of 8	68	78	92,984	International	Verdi	Yankees
1966	Mud Hens	6 of 8	71	75	124,048	International	Babe	Yankees
1967	Mud Hens	3 of 8	73	66	94,308	International	Tighe	Tigers
1968	Mud Hens	1 of 8	83	64	113,098	International	Tighe	Tigers
1969	Mud Hens	6 of 8	68	72	100,493	International	Tighe	Tigers
1970	Mud Hens	8 of 8	51	89	86,428	International	Carswell	Tigers
1971	Mud Hens	7 of 8	60	80	88,438	International	Roarke	Tigers
1972	Mud Hens	5 of 8	75	69	100,171	International	Lipon	Tigers
1973	Mud Hens	4 of 4	65	81	92,366	International	Lipon, Deal	Tigers
1974	Mud Hens	3 of 4	70	74	93,384	International	Bunning	Phillies
1975	Mud Hens	7 of 8	62	78	103,189	International	Bunning	Phillies
1976	Mud Hens	8 of 8	55	85	106,106	International	Sparks	Indians
1977	Mud Hens	8 of 8	56	84	102,606	International	Cassini	Indians
1978	Mud Hens	3 of 8	74	66	163,651	International	Ermer	Twins
1979	Mud Hens	7 of 8	63	76	148,592	International	Ermer	Twins
1980	Mud Hens	2 of 8	77	63	210,685	International	Ermer	Twins
1981	Mud Hens	8 of 8	53	87	170,359	International	Ermer	Twins
1982	Mud Hens	7 of 8	60	80	150,184	International	Ermer	Twins
1983	Mud Hens	5 of 8	68	72	164,269	International	Ermer	Twins
1984	Mud Hens	3 of 8	74	63	182,247	International	Ermer	Twins
1985	Mud Hens	6 of 8	71	68	167,787	International	Ermer	Twins
1986	Mud Hens	6 of 8	62	77	145,809	International	Manuel	Twins
1987	Mud Hens	5 of 8	70	70	194,001	International	Roberts	Tigers
1988	Mud Hens	4 of 4	58	84	193,101	International	Corrales	Tigers
1989	Mud Hens	4 of 4	69	76	182,744	International	Wockenfuss	Tigers
1990	Mud Hens	4 of 4	58	86	168,018	International	Wockenfuss, Gamboa	Tigers

Year	Team	Finish	W	L	Attendance	League	Manager	Affliliate
1991	Mud Hens	3 of 4	74	70	229,419	International	Sparks	Tigers
1992	Mud Hens	3 of 4	64	80	254,723	International	Sparks	Tigers
1993	Mud Hens	5 of 5	65	77	285,155	International	Sparks	Tigers
1994	Mud Hens	5 of 5	63	79	304,827	International	Sparks, Parrish	Tigers
1995	Mud Hens	4 of 5	71	71	306,906	International	Runnells	Tigers
1996	Mud Hens	3 of 5	70	72	316,126	International	Runnells	Tigers
1997	Mud Hens	5 of 5	68	73	325,532	International	Ezell, Roof	Tigers
1998	Mud Hens	4 of 4	52	89	311,652	International	Roof	Tigers
1999	Mud Hens	4 of 4	57	87	295,173	International	Roof	Tigers
2000	Mud Hens	4 of 4	55	86	298,564	International	Anderson, Ezell	Tigers
2001	Mud Hens	4 of 4	65	79	300,079	International	Fields	Tigers
2002	Mud Hens	1 of 4	81	63	547,204	International	Fields	Tigers
2003	Mud Hens					International	Parrish	Tigers

This racetrack grandstand served the same function along the third base side of the field when the track was converted for baseball in 1965. (Photo reprinted with permission of *The Toledo Blade*.)

A former racetrack, The Fort Miami Fairgrounds on Key Street in Maumee was hastily converted into a ball park in the spring of 1965 and is shown here in 1966. Lucas County had secured a franchise, and the team needed a place to play—and in a hurry. The complex at the Lucas County Recreation Center featured a fine playing field, and provided an intimate relationship between the game and its spectators. The facilities were another matter, however. Locker rooms, training facilities, and offices for the teams were woefully inadequate. The dugouts had no running water, and players had to make their way through waiting fans when they made their way to and from the locker room. The fans also suffered, as rest rooms and concessions were often over crowded and away from the field. In spite of its inadequacies, the park was in service for 37 seasons. (Photo reprinted with permission of *The Toledo Blade*.)

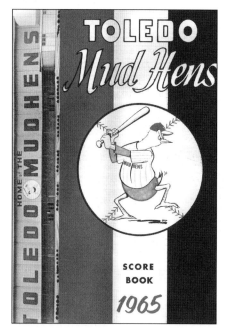

After a nine-year absence, baseball had a new beginning in northwest Ohio as the Mud Hens returned in 1965. There was also a new Mud Hen logo. Created by Gabriel "Gabe" Pinciotti, the new version was less the long pants of its predecessor and looked like "a skinny chicken with a beer belly," according to its designer. The team logo is now a part of countless clothing and souvenir items and known world wide. The Mud Hen merchandise line is the best selling in all of minor league sports. (Arnold Bunge, Jr. collection.)

Mike Hegan, Toledo Mud Hens' first baseman, takes a cut at the Lucas County Recreation Center during the 1965 season. This was the first year of play at the county owned facility, and the first of two for Hegan as a Mud Hen. He became the regular first baseman in 1966 and led the league in triples and walks. The son of long time Cleveland Indians catcher Jim Hegan would go on to a 14-year major league career, mostly as a part-time player. This was also the first of the two-year working agreement with the New York Yankees. The Mud Hens did not fare particularly well, finishing seventh and then sixth in the eight team International League. The Yankees were not doing well themselves, suffering through the worst winning drought in their history, and delighting Yankee haters with a last place finish in 1966. (Photo reprinted with permission of *The Toledo Blade*.)

Bobby Murcer was at shortstop for Toledo when they were the top farm club of the New York Yankees in 1966. His finest day as a Mud Hen came on June 26 when he hit four consecutive home runs in a doubleheader (two in each game) against the Toronto Maple Leafs at the Lucas County Recreation Center. A scant Sunday crowd of 755 witnessed his feat. Murcer went on to an all-star career with the Yankees, Giants, and Cubs that spanned 17 seasons. He duplicated his feat of hitting four consecutive home runs in a single day in the major leagues when he did so in a doubleheader for the New York Yankees on June 24, 1970. (Photo reprinted with permission of *The Toledo Blade*.)

Jim Rooker had one of Toledo's best ever clutch pitching performances in beating Columbus as the Mud Hens claimed the Governor's Cup in 1967. Rooker allowed no hits over seven innings, and finished with a one-hitter in the 1–0 win in the deciding game. He struck out ten Jets. Rooker became a dominating pitcher for the Hens the following season as he helped them to the pennant with a 14–8 record. His 206 strikeouts were the most made by a Toledo pitcher since Gene Conley's 211 in 1953, and have not been topped since. Rooker went on to a 13-year major league career. (Photo reprinted with permission of *The Toledo Blade*.)

The 1968 edition of the Mud Hens won the only pennant of the Maumee Era, and they did so by winning more games—83—than any other Toledo team since baseball returned to the area in 1965. Pitching led the way as Mike Marshall and Toledoan Dick Drago set the Maumee Era record for wins with 15 each and Jim Rooker set the Maumee Era record for strikeouts with 206. Fred Scherman's earned run average of 1.76 is the lowest ever by a Toledo pitcher with over 100 innings pitched. Twelve Mud Hen pitchers from the 1968 team went on to the major leagues, and several had long and noteworthy careers. Jack Tighe was named the International League and Minor League Manager of the Year. Pictured from left to right are: (front row) bat boy Jeff Nicholas, Dick Drago, Bob Christian, Bill Fulk, Marty Richardson, Fred Scherman, Mike Marshall, and bat boy Joe Caponigro; (middle row) Mike Derrick, Ike Brown, coach Stubby Overmire, manager Jack Tighe, Jim Rooker, Ron Woods, Arlo Brunsberg, Lennie Green, and Les Cain; (back row) trainer Doc Foley, Junior Lopez, Tom Timmerman, Dick Radatz, Leo Marentette, Don Pepper, Dave Campbell, Jack DiLauro, Mike Kilkenny, and general manager Charlie Senger. (The Toledo Mud Hens.)

Opposite: The 1967 Toledo Mud Hens won the Governor's Cup after finishing in third place during the regular season. Toledo defeated Richmond three games to two and Columbus four games to one to take the Cup. This remains the only Governor's Cup that Toledo has ever won. It came in the first season that Toledo was affiliated with the Detroit Tigers since baseball had returned to Toledo in 1965. Jack Tighe was named the International League Manager of the Year and Tom Matchick was selected for the all-star team. Pictured from left to right are: (front row) batboy Terry Kwiatkowski, Bob Reed, Wayne Comer, Jim Rooker, Ron Woods, Joe Brauer, Ron Chandler, and Fritz Fisher; (middle row) batboy Joe Bauer, Dave Campbell, Dick Drago, Ike Brown, manager Jack Tighe, Arlo Brunsberg, and Art Todtenhausen; (back row) trainer Doc Foley, Jack DiLauro, Tom Timmerman, Don Pepper, Dave Wissman, Chris Cannizzaro, Don Dillard, Junior Lopez, Leo Marentette, and clubhouse attendant Jim Schmakel. Absent was Daryl Patterson as well as several of the Hens—Pat Dobson, John Hiller, George Korince, Fred Lasher, Mike Marshall, and Matchick—who had been called up to the Detroit Tigers for their pennant push that fell just one game short. (Photo reprinted with permission of *The Toledo Blade*.)

Jack Tighe, Mud Hens manager, in his 1951 uniform featuring and Old English "T" on the cap, similar to the parent Detroit Tiger uniform. Tighe is one of only four Toledo managers of two seasons or more to have a winning record. His 294-284 won-lost record trails only Charlie Strobel's 497-402, Charlie Morton's 219-180, and George Selkirk's 236-201. (Photo reprinted with permission of *The Toledo Blade*.)

Jack Tighe, shown in this 1968 photo, managed for Toledo in two different eras, and both times the Mud Hens were affiliated with the Detroit Tigers. In 1951 the Mud Hens played in the American Association, finishing sixth, fading after a fast start. In first place early in the season, Tighe responded to a suggestion that his team would falter in true Yogi-fashion, "We always attempt to take care of the present immediately and worry about the future when it's present." He returned to manage the Tigers' International League entry for three seasons with rare success. His 1967 squad finished in a rush and won Toledo's only Governor's Cup championship. The following season the Mud Hens won their first, and still only, International League pennant. Jack Tighe died in 2002 after spending 52 years in organized baseball. (Photo reprinted with permission of *The Toledo Blade*.)

Gene Cook made the Mud Hens go! Made their general manager in 1978, he saw their attendance grow from an average of less than 100,000 per year before his arrival to consistently over 300,000 annually. He did it by promotions. *USA Today Baseball Weekly* said that Cook accomplished "one of the great public relations moves in the history of minor league baseball" when he enlisted Toledoan Jamie Farr's M*A*S*H character Max Klinger to incorporate support for

the Mud Hens in the popular television show. This made the already well-known Mud Hens "a household name around the world." He may have given the Mud Hens even a bigger boost in popularity when he led the way for their return to downtown Toledo. Gene Cook had the vision that the future growth of professional baseball in Toledo depended on a new downtown ball park. He worked to make it happen and it has. Indications are, after the first year's successes in 2002, that this may be his best promotion of all. (Photo reprinted with permission of *The Toledo Blade*.)

Jamie Farr has always been a tireless supporter and promoter of his Toledo hometown. Farr began spreading the word about the Mud Hens as he incorporated them into the M*A*S*H television show through his character Klinger in the seventies and eighties, helping to make the Mud Hens name known the world over. He was on hand to emcee the Fifth Third Field groundbreaking on October 20, 2000 and is a part of every Mud Hen home game via video messages on Fifth Third Field's huge scoreboard. (The Toledo Mud Hens.)

With Cal Ermer at the helm, the 1980 Mud Hens finished second to Columbus in the International League standings. In the playoffs, Toledo defeated Rochester three games to one, but lost to Columbus four games to one in the Governor's Cup finals. Toledo placed three players—Dave Engle, Greg Johnston, and Ray Smith—on the International League All-Star team and drew a Maumee Era record of 210,685 through the turnstiles. A fine season could have been outstanding if Toledo would have played better against Columbus. Besides losing to the Clippers in the playoffs, the Hens dropped 16 of 20 regular season games to the team from the capital city of Ohio. Pictured from left to right are: (front row) unknown, Buck Chamberlin, Johnny Walker, Kurt Seibert, Ron Washington, manager Cal Ermer, Bob Veselic, Tom Brueggemann, and unknown; (middle row) Wally Sarmiento, Bruce MacPherson, Ray Smith, Greg Johnston, unknown, Randy Bush, Les Pearsey, and Mike Bacsik; (back row) Jim Rohr, Dave Engle, Steve Herz, Tom Chism, Gary Serum, Mike Kinnunen, Al Williams, Fernando Arroyo, Gary Ward, Steve Douglas(?), Jesus Vega, and general manager Gene Cook. (The Toledo Mud Hens.)

Dave Engle, Mud Hen third baseman, won the 1980 International League batting title by the closest possible margin with a .307 average. Engel was locked in a duel with Wade Boggs of Pawtucket as the two teams faced each other on the season's final day. It was not until Wade Boggs was retired on the season's last swing that Engle could claim the title. (The Toledo Mud Hens.)

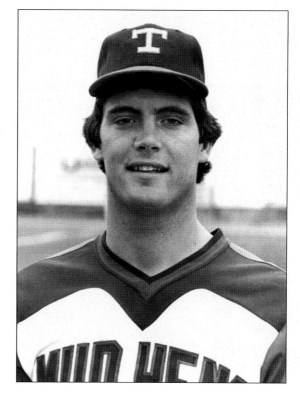

Greg "Boomer" Wells played only one year for the Mud Hens, but what a year it was. In 1982, the Twins farmhand was the International League's leading hitter with a .336 average and was named to the circuit's All-Star team. He also led the league with 107 runs batted in and chipped in 28 home runs, narrowly missing the triple crown while playing first base. He received the "Star of Stars" award as shown here for dominating the league's batting statistics. In 1983, Wells began an outstanding career in Japan. There he ranks number four on the all-time career batting average list at .317. He also won a triple crown and twice was MVP of the Japanese All-Star game. (Photo reprinted with permission of *The Toledo Blade*.)

Outfielder Tack Wilson's first of two years in Toledo was 1983, when he had the fourth highest International League batting average at .325 and stole 53 bases. His steals were the most by a Mud Hen for a season in the Maumee Era. He followed in 1984 with .287 and 48 steals, this time leading the league in that department. (The Toledo Mud Hens.)

Tim Teufel was the International League's Most Valuable Player and All-Star second baseman in 1983. Teufel hit for both average and power, batting .323 with 27 home runs and 100 runs batted in. He set a Maumee Era record with 103 runs scored. Teufel, who also played in Toledo in 1982, went on to an 11-year major league career with the Twins, Mets, and Padres. (Photo reprinted with permission of *The Toledo Blade*.)

Brad Havens was the International League's Most Valuable Pitcher and All-Star team starting pitcher for the 1984 season. Havens won 11 and lost 10 with the league's second best earned run average of 2.61 while leading the league with 12 complete games and 169 strikeouts. Brad pitched for the Mud Hens in 1983, 1984, and 1989 and played eight seasons in the major leagues with the Twins, Orioles, Dodgers, Indians, and Tigers. (Photo reprinted with permission of *The Toledo Blade*.)

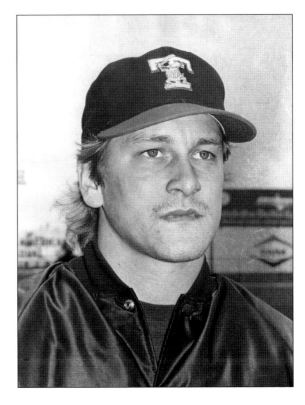

Nobody has managed more Toledo baseball games than Cal Ermer. Managing the Mud Hens for the Minnesota Twins for eight seasons, the popular skipper won more games and lost more games that any other Toledo manager as well. The only Toledo manager to be at the helm for more than 1,000 games never won a pennant but guided the Hens to three Governor's Cup berths. Ermer, a former Twins manager himself, had a hand in developing the Minnesota talent that won the World Series in 1987. (Photo reprinted with permission of *The Toledo Blade*.)

Outfielder Andre David played five seasons (1982–1986) for the Mud Hens. Three of those seasons were as an everyday player. He capped his career here by winning the International League batting championship with a .328 average in 1986. (The Toledo Mud Hens.)

Steve Searcy was the International League's Most Valuable Pitcher and All-Star team starting pitcher for the 1988 season. Searcy went 13-7 with a 2.59 earned run average while leading the league with 176 strikeouts. His win total tied for the league lead. Searcy pitched for Toledo from 1987 through 1990 and, despite this batting pose, never had an at bat for Toledo. (The Toledo Mud Hens.)

Willie Hernandez, the Detroit Tiger pitcher, was sent to Toledo for rehabilitation during the 1987 season. He had previously been a Mud Hen as a starting pitcher in 1975. This Detroit Tiger relief pitcher won the Cy Young Award as the American League's best pitcher in 1984. (The Toledo Mud Hens.)

Kirk Gibson was a Mud Hen, also on a rehabilitation assignment from the Tigers, for only six games during the 1987 season. Gibson played 17 years in the major leagues, 12 of them in Detroit. He was briefly with the Royals and Pirates, and was the National League's Most Valuable Player for the Dodgers in 1988. His speed and aggressive and gutsy play made him a fan favorite wherever he played. (The Toledo Mud Hens.)

Ned Skeldon, the man who brought baseball back to the Toledo area, is shown here with his wife, Sue. The occasion is the dedication of the Lucas County Recreation Center ball park, as Ned Skeldon Stadium on June 28, 1988. Toledo's long and rich baseball tradition had been interrupted for nine seasons beginning in 1956. The Toledo Sox, owned by the Milwaukee Braves, were suddenly and surprisingly moved to Wichita, Kansas following the 1955 season. Then vice-mayor of Toledo, Skeldon realized that a new team could not be had without a place to play. He made an offer to purchase Swayne Field and helped place a bond issue before the voters for a new stadium. Both were rejected, and Swayne Field was razed in 1956. Ned Skeldon then labored for a decade to return baseball to the Toledo community. He didn't do it alone, but according to *The Toledo Blade*, "Mr. Skeldon provided the motivating force and the liaison direction for the operation." Baseball was played at the county-owned facility for 37 seasons because Ned Skeldon saw to it. Skeldon, a lifelong public servant, also served as president of the Mud Hens for three years. (Photo reprinted with permission of *The Toledo Blade*.)

Jose Lima pitched the only official no-hitter (nine innings) by a Mud Hen in Ned Skeldon Stadium/Lucas County Recreation Center. On August 17, 1994 he beat Pawtucket 3–0 in a night game before 5,461. Lima struck out 13 and allowed only one base runner. He gave up a walk leading off the eighth inning, just missing a perfect game. (The Toledo Mud Hens.)

Phil Hiatt was the International League's Most Valuable Player and All-Star third baseman in 1996. During his only season in Toledo, he established Maumee Era records with 42 home runs and 119 runs batted in. His home run total was the highest in the International League in 38 seasons and second only to Jerry Witte's 46 on the all-time Toledo list. (The Toledo Mud Hens.)

Eddie Gaillard led the International League in saves for the 1997 season and was the All-Star team relief pitcher. His 28 saves established the all-time Toledo record. (The Toledo Mud Hens.)

Bubba Trammell played in Toledo for only parts of two seasons, 1996 and 1997. In spite of his short stay on the way to the majors, he left his mark in both the Toledo and the International League record books. In only 90 games in 1997, he belted 28 home runs, good for a tie for seventh place on Toledo's all-time single season home run list. On August 9, he became only the eighth player in more than a century of International League history to hit four home runs in a game. His last swing of the game won for the Hens in the bottom of the 13th inning at Ned Skeldon Stadium. (Photo reprinted with permission of *The Toledo Blade*.)

Dave McCarty led the 1999 Mud Hens in several hitting categories with 132 games, 466 at bats, 85 runs scored, 125 hits, and 31 home runs. His 31 home runs rank number five on Toledo's all-time list behind Jerry Witte's 46 in 1946; Phil Hiatt's 42 in 1996; George Crowe's 34 in 1954; and Hal Trosky's 33 in 1933. The fine-fielding first baseman also led the 1999 Mud Hens to the all-time Toledo season home run record. (The Toledo Mud Hens.)

The 1999 Toledo Mud Hens seem to be having fun here. They didn't play well, finishing last in their division and with the worst record in the 14 team International League, but they hit more home runs—176—than any other team in Toledo history. They eclipsed the record of the 1996 team that hit 165 to top the 163 hit by the 1954 Toledo Sox. Leading the way in 1999 were: Dave McCarty 31, Gabe Alvarez 21, Pat Lennon 21, Jason Maxwell 15, Kimera Bartee 12, and Ricky Cradle and Pedro Swann with 10 each. Pictured from left to right are: (front row) Jose Macias, Robinson Checo, Nelson Cruz, Bryan Corey, Muddy the Mud Hen, Luis Polonia, Jason Maxwell, and Brian Looney; (middle row) Mike Grzanich, Dave Borkowski, Walt McKeel, pitching coach Dan Warthen, manager Gene Roof, hitting coach Skeeter Barnes, Gabe Alvarez, Joe Siddall, and Pedro Swann; (back row) trainer Lon Pinhey, strength and conditioning coach Brian Jordan, Rickey Cradel, Willis Roberts, Jim Bonnici, Dave McCarty, Matt Drews, Will Bunson, Brandon Reed, Jose Alberro, Kimera Bartee, and Gabe Kapler. (The Toledo Mud Hens)

Billy McMillon's .345 batting average won the International League batting title in 2000. He had an 18-game hitting streak and posted 32 multi-hit games during his only season as a Mud Hen. The Toledo outfielder's average was the highest of any player during the Maumee Era, and he was named to the league All-Star team. (The Toledo Mud Hens.)

The former Lucas County Recreation Center was renamed in 1988 in honor of Ned Skeldon, who was largely responsible for the return of baseball to northwestern Ohio. The park became affectionately known as "The Ned." The final game at Ned Skeldon Stadium was September 3, 2001. (The Toledo Mud Hens.)

Four
The Coming Home Era
2002

THEY'RE BACK. The Mud Hens came home to Toledo in 2002, and what a return it was! They came to a new place to play in the heart of the city, to the finest minor league ballpark in America. They came to play well and were a rare winning team. They came to play before big crowds. There was unprecedented fan support. All this made for a dream baseball season that rewarded the long faithful, and brought many newcomers to witness and be a part of professional baseball in Toledo.

Technically, the Mud Hens had not played a game in Toledo in 50 years. The Mud Hens left town in 1952, but were replaced in 1953 by the Sox. The Sox left after the 1955 season, and there was no baseball until the Mud Hens returned to Maumee in 1965 to stay through 2001. So for the first time since June of 1952, Toledo had a team called the Mud Hens playing in the city.

Toledo's new park, Fifth Third Field, is located downtown and just a few blocks down Monroe Street from Toledo's very first park. The park is nestled into the warehouse district with century-old structures incorporated into the complex. Spectator accommodations were a priority in planning and design. The seats were computer aligned to face the center of the diamond and are located near the action. The main concourse encircles the playing field allowing fans to enjoy every feature of the park—concession stands, the largest souvenir store in minor league baseball, and the huge scoreboard—all while keeping an eye on the game. The field itself is asymmetrical and incorporates features of some favorite, older major league parks. It has character. The player facilities and those provided for administering the business of baseball are also major improvements.

The Erie Sea Wolves, the Tigers Class AA affiliate, had a very successful 2001 season. Many from that team graduated to Toledo for 2002 and provided the core of the Mud Hens team. Credit the parent Detroit Tigers with keeping the roster full. The result was consistent good play and a yearlong battle with Louisville for the West Division championship, captured by the Mud Hens in the final days.

The whole community supported the Mud Hens new deal; labor, business, government, and the public all came together. The fans came out in numbers never before seen and greatly exceeded expectations. Later in the season, when it became evident what was going on in downtown Toledo, sellouts became the norm.

The first season of the Coming Home Era was successful in every respect; almost magical.

The Toledo Mud Hens, champions of the West Division of the International League for 2002, pose at their new home in downtown Toledo. It has been jokingly said that this team ruined Toledo's reputation by winning. Pictured from left to right are: (front row) trainer Matt Rankin, Chad Alexander, Omar Infante, Andres Torres, Jarrod Patterson, Jamie Walker, Craig Monroe, Eric Munson, Ryan Jackson, and strength coach Jeff Kearse; (middle row) Craig Wilson, hitting coach Leon Durham, Adam Bernero, Tim Kalita, Eric Eckenstahler, Oscar Henriquez, Mike Maroth, Julio Santana, manager Bruce Fields, and pitching coach Jeff Jones; (top row) Brian Rios, Chris Wakeland, Matt Perisho, Kris Keller, Shane Loux, Matt Walbeck, Oscar Salazar, Brian Powell, and Brandon Inge. (The Toledo Mud Hens.)

Eric Munson provided much of the power hitting that was a part of the Toledo Mud Hens' 2002 championship season. He led the club with 24 home runs and 84 runs batted in as well as in games played with 136. Munson accomplished a rarity when he had two home runs in an inning. He accomplished the feat during an eight run outburst in the second inning on July 24 as Pat Ahearne shut out Rochester 8–0 at Fifth Third Field. Only once before did a Mud Hen have two home runs in an inning—that was by Tom Matchick on July 1, 1967. (The Toledo Mud Hens.)

Nate Cornejo delivers here, and was one of the mainstays of the fine Mud Hen pitching staff that had much to do with the team's on field success in 2002. The second-year Hen won nine games, was a close number two on the staff in strikeouts, and was a part of the starting rotation all season long. Cornejo had an outstanding 20–7 combined record in 2001 with Erie, Toledo, and Detroit. (The Toledo Mud Hens.)

Mud Hen Manager and third base coach Bruce Fields greets and congratulates center fielder Andres Torres as he rounds third and heads for home. Fields guided the Hens to the International League West Division title in his second season as the Toledo manager. Fields won three batting championships in his 14-year playing career and has been a coach and manager in the Detroit Tiger organization since 1992. The speedster Torres led the Mud Hens in triples (8), runs scored (80), and stolen bases (42). (The Toledo Mud Hens.)

The Mud Hens players celebrate with their fans after winning the 2002 International League West Division championship. The Mud Hens won out over the Louisville Bats after engaging in a season long race with the Cincinnati Reds' top farm club. The rare championship, coupled with the new park, sparked unprecedented fan interest that resulted in an unimaginably successful dream season. (The Toledo Mud Hens.)

Joe Napoli became general manager of the Toledo Mud Hens in 1999, after serving in management positions with the Mud Hens twice, the Chicago Bulls, the Detroit Tigers, and the Canton-Akron Indians. He got more than one job, however. He was charged with operating the Maumee Era club and was immediately involved in the move back to Toledo from the conceptual level. He was running a business and overseeing the construction of a $39 million stadium at the same time. A tireless worker, a juggler of many balls, and able to satisfy the many facets of a business that involves the private sector, government, and the public, his efforts have paid off with the magnificent successes of the Toledo Mud Hens 2002 season. (The Toledo Mud Hens.)

The Toledo radio team of Jim Weber and Frank Gilhooley are fixtures in the Toledo broadcast booth. Gilhooley began his baseball radio broadcasts for the Toledo Sox in 1953. He broadcast all three Sox seasons. When baseball returned to Toledo in 1965, Gilhooley was once again the voice of the team. After a few years he left to become Sports Director at Channel 13 where he televised some Hens games. He retired from television in 1986 and returned to radio where he remains as partner to Jim Weber. During the 2002 season, Gilhooley celebrated his 50th anniversary of Toledo baseball radio broadcasting. Weber began broadcasting Toledo baseball in 1975. In his 28 seasons he has not missed a game! His streak of 3,409 consecutive games broadcast through the 2002 season is most probably unmatched in minor league history. Weber doubles as the Hens' travel secretary. (The Toledo Mud Hens.)

Muddy the Mud Hen, who appears at every home game and at community events as mascot and ambassador of the club, is shown here saluting fans at Fifth Third Field. Muddy, a favorite of fans of all ages, has appeared in various forms over the years and never speaks. (The Toledo Mud Hens.)

Named the best minor league ball park in America by *Newsweek* magazine, Fifth Third Field opened its turnstiles and ushered in the Coming Home Era on April 9, 2002. Nestled into Toledo's warehouse district near downtown (south side), and bordered by St. Clair, Washington, Huron, and Monroe Streets, the new park welcomes baseball back to the heart of the city. Fifth Third Field is just a few blocks away from Toledo's first baseball home, League Park, which also stood on Monroe Street beginning in 1883. The opening day overflow crowd shown here was one of 27 sellouts during the record breaking inaugural season. Toledo fans set a new standard as season attendance reached 547,204 at 71 home games. The season total was an increase of 82.4 percent over the 300,079 attendance at Ned Skeldon Stadium in Maumee in 2001. The old mark of 343,614 had been held by fans of the 1953 Sox who played at Swayne Field, also on Monroe Street. (The Toledo Mud Hens.)

Looking north over Fifth Third Field, the Maumee River is seen disappearing into Lake Erie. (The Toledo Mud Hens.)

FIVE
Heroes

TOLEDO HAS BEEN a significant contributor to the American national game from the very time professional baseball began in the city. The baseball people that have made some of these contributions are the heroes of this chapter. These are people with Toledo connections who have excelled at the game's highest level and have been recognized as among the very best that baseball has ever seen.

Foremost among the Toledo heroes are those enshrined in baseball's Hall of Fame. These number fifteen, of which ten have passed through Toledo on their way to outstanding careers in the major leagues. They are Casey Stengel, Roger Bresnahan, Addie Joss, Bill Terry, Joe McCarthy, Freddie Lindstrom, Kirby Puckett, Hack Wilson, Dazzy Vance, and Jocko Conlan. Five others have come to Toledo after earning their Hall of Fame credentials—Oscar Charleston, Elmer Flick, Turkey Stearnes, Billy Evans, and Jim Bunning.

Former Toledo players are the holders of some significant baseball records. Three former Mud Hens have won the Cy Young Award as the best pitcher in their league for a season (see page 116). A significant first was accomplished when Toledo's Moses Fleetwood Walker became the first black man to play in the major leagues in 1884. Deacon McGuire, a Toledo catcher in 1884, holds an endurance record of playing 26 major league seasons, more than any other non-pitcher who ever played the game. Scores of other less significant records are also held by Toledo players. Examples include Ray Chapman's major league record of 67 sacrifices in a season or Roy Grimes batting in a run in 17 consecutive games, and Frank Torre scoring six times in a game for a National league record. Some made the record book instantly, like Chuck Tanner who hit a home run on the first pitch he saw in the majors. Not all are positive though, as Terry Felton's record 16 straight losses at the beginning of his career attests.

Since 1902, Toledo teams have played at the highest minor league level, just a step away from the major leagues. Many Toledo players were, then, just a step away from the major leagues. This was especially true before major league expansion began in 1961.

Of the approximately 2,506 players to wear a Toledo uniform, about 1,700 have made that step to the big time. The 38 Toledo-born players who have played at baseball's highest level are outlined on page 118. Former Toledo baseballists have excelled not only as players, but also as umpires and managers. Jocko Conlan is a former Mud Hen player who has been elected to the Hall of Fame as an umpire. Hank O'Day is another that should be. Toledo has had a disproportionate number of alumni succeed as major league managers in terms of tenure, winning, and championships.

There are some who qualify as double heroes, like Roger Bresnahan who not only made it to the major leagues, but also is the only Toledo native son enshrined in the Hall of Fame. Another is Hack Wilson, a Hall of Fame player who holds a significant record with his 191 runs-batted-in during a season.

The last of our heroes is pioneer baseball researcher Ralph Elliott Lin Weber. Lin Weber devoted a lifetime to researching and documenting all facets of Toledo baseball and its history. Before the advent of the personal computer, and in spite of being deaf, he compiled huge amounts of data and was a contributor to the first baseball encyclopedia.

CHARLES DILLON "CASEY" STENGEL was elected to the Hall of Fame in 1966 as a manager (he also played 14 years). While managing at Toledo from 1926 through 1931, he won 490 games while losing 498, and led the Mud Hens to the pennant and its only Junior World Series win in 1927. As a pinch hitter and outfielder, he batted .322 in 155 games. He later guided the New York Yankees to ten pennants and seven World Series championships in a 12-year span highlighting a 25-year major league managing career. (National Baseball Hall of Fame and Library, Cooperstown, N.Y.)

Casey Stengel, Toledo, 1926–1931 (Robert Koehler.)

ROGER PHILIP BRESNAHAN was elected to the Hall of Fame in 1945 as a catcher. He made his professional debut with the Mud Hens in 1898 as a pitcher. He was the Owner and President of the Toledo club from 1916 through 1923. Bresnahan also managed the Mud Hens from 1916 through 1920 winning 283 and losing 362. As an occasional player, he batted .262 in 112 games as a catcher and outfielder. Roger Bresnahan is the only native Toledoan enshrined in the Hall of Fame. The New York Giant leadoff man formed one of baseball's greatest all-time batteries with Christy Mathewson. He played all nine positions during his career. He later managed the Cardinals and Cubs and coached for the Tigers. (National Baseball Hall of Fame and Library, Cooperstown, N.Y.)

Roger Bresnahan, Toledo, 1898, 1916–1923 (Marian Childers.)

WILLIAM HAROLD "BILL" TERRY was elected in 1954 as a first baseman. Terry came to Toledo as a pitcher for the 1922 season, staying for two years. As a pitcher he won nine and lost nine, but because of his potent bat, he was moved to first base. As a 25 year old, he managed the Mud Hens for part of the 1923 season and hit the ball at a .377 clip. During his 14-year major league career with the New York Giants, he had a .341 batting average, the highest ever for a National League left-handed hitter. He is the last player to hit .400 in the National League, and also managed the Giants for ten seasons as the great John McGraw's successor. (Photo File, Inc.)

Bill Terry, Toledo, 1922–1923 (Robert Koehler.)

ADRIAN "ADDIE" JOSS was elected to the Hall of Fame in 1978 as a pitcher. While at Toledo for the 1900 and 1901 seasons, he won 46 games. Joss made his home in Toledo and was a sportswriter for *The Toledo News Bee*. His major league career, all at Cleveland, was brilliant, but cut short by death due to tubercular meningitis at age 31. Joss, along with fellow Hall of Fame member Roger Bresnahan, is buried in Toledo's historic Woodlawn Cemetery. His career earned run average of 1.88 is second among all pitchers ever. He won 160 games in nine seasons, including 45 by shutout, and one perfect game. (National Baseball Hall of Fame and Library, Cooperstown, N.Y.)

JOSEPH VINCENT "JOE" MCCARTHY was elected to the Hall of Fame in 1957 as a manager. McCarthy played at Toledo from 1908 through 1911, primarily as an infielder batting .231 in 350 games. He never made it to the major leagues as a player, but managed 24 big league seasons. McCarthy has the highest winning percentage in baseball history, winning nine pennants and finishing second seven times. With the Cubs, Yankees, and Red Sox, he never had a losing season nor finished in the second division. (National Baseball Hall of Fame and Library, Cooperstown, N.Y.)

FREDERICK CHARLES "FREDDIE" LINDSTROM was elected to the Hall of Fame in 1976 as a third baseman. Lindstrom was a 16-year-old third baseman for Toledo in 1922 and was also a Mud Hen in 1923. He batted .272 in 165 games for the two years. He went on to be a fixture at third base for great New York Giant teams led by John McGraw, and became the youngest player ever to play in a World Series in 1924 at age 18. (National Baseball Hall of Fame and Library, Cooperstown, N.Y.)

Freddie Lindstrom, Toledo, 1922–1923 (Robert Koehler.)

OSCAR MCKINLEY CHARLESTON was elected to the Hall of Fame in 1976 as center fielder, first baseman, and manager. Charleston managed and played first base for the 1939 Toledo Crawfords, who played in both the Negro National League and the Negro American League, the two major Negro leagues of the time. Charleston is regarded by many as the finest all-around player in Negro League history. (National Baseball Hall of Fame and Library, Cooperstown, N.Y.)

ELMER HARRISON FLICK was elected to the Hall of Fame in 1963 as a right fielder. Flick came to Toledo in 1911 following a 13-year major league career. In two seasons as a Mud Hen outfielder, he batted .291 in 199 games. He was one of baseball's best hitters at the turn of the century, batting .315 for his major league career. Flick possessed good speed, and led the American League in triples three years in a row and twice in steals. He was so highly thought of that Cleveland refused to trade him even for Ty Cobb. (National Baseball Hall of Fame and Library, Cooperstown, N.Y.)

NORMAN THOMAS "TURKEY" STEARNES was elected to the Hall of Fame in 2000 as a center fielder. He captained the 1945 Toledo Cubs of the United States Baseball League, a minor Negro league. Stearnes was a prolific home run hitter and led the Negro National League in round-trippers six times with the Detroit Stars. (National Baseball Hall of Fame and Library, Cooperstown, N.Y.)

KIRBY PUCKETT was elected to the Hall of Fame in 2001 as a center fielder. He played at Toledo in 1984, batting .263 in 21 games. Puckett was an all-star 10 of his 12 seasons with the Minnesota Twins. He had a career batting average of .318, won six Gold Gloves, and led the Twins to two World Series titles before his career was cut short by glaucoma. (National Baseball Hall of Fame and Library, Cooperstown, N.Y.)

JOHN BERTRAND "JOCKO" CONLAN was elected to the Hall of Fame in 1974 as an umpire. Conlan batted .290 in 69 games as a Toledo Mud Hen outfielder during the 1930 season. Conlan played two seasons for the Chicago White Sox and then went on to umpire 24 years in the National League. He earned respect for how he called and controlled games. He umpired six World Series and six all-star games. (National Baseball Hall of Fame and Library, Cooperstown, N.Y.)

Jocko Conlan, Toledo, 1930 (Robert Koehler.)

CLARENCE ARTHUR "DAZZY" VANCE was elected to the Hall of Fame in 1955 as a pitcher. Vance played ten years in the minor leagues before reaching the major leagues at age 31, and had a lackluster record of two wins and six losses at Toledo in 1917. Despite his late start, he won 197 games in the National League and was the highest paid pitcher in history at $25,000 in 1929. (National Baseball Hall of Fame and Library, Cooperstown, N.Y.)

Dazzy Vance, Toledo, 1917 (Photo reprinted with permission of *The Toledo Blade*.)

LEWIS ROBERT "HACK" WILSON was elected to the Hall of Fame in 1979 as a center fielder. Wilson played in 55 games for Toledo in 1925 batting .343. In a short 12-year major league career, he won four home run titles. His career was capped by his 1930 season when he averaged .356 had 56 home runs and drove in 191 runs—a record that still stands. (National Baseball Hall of Fame and Library, Cooperstown, N.Y.)

JAMES PAUL DAVID "JIM" BUNNING was elected to the Hall of Fame in 1996 as a pitcher. Bunning managed the Mud Hens during the 1974 and 1975 seasons for the Phillies organization, winning 132 and losing 152. As a major league pitcher, mostly for the Tigers and Phillies, he won more than 100 games and struck out more than 1,000 in both major leagues. He is one of only two pitchers to throw a no-hitter in each league. The no-hitter in the National League was a perfect game in 1964. It was the first perfect game in the league since the two games pitched in 1880 by Lee Richmond and Montie Ward, which came five days apart. Richmond was a Toledoan and is buried in Forest Cemetery. (National Baseball Hall of Fame and Library, Cooperstown, N.Y.)

WILLIAM GEORGE "BILLY" EVANS was elected to the Hall of Fame in 1973 as an umpire. Evans served Toledo as General Manager in 1932 and again as president from 1949 through 1951 while the Detroit Tigers owned the Mud Hens. Before coming to Toledo, Evans was the youngest man ever to umpire in the major leagues and worked in blue in the American League from 1906 until 1927. After Toledo, he was General Manager at Detroit and Cleveland. (National Baseball Hall of Fame and Library, Cooperstown, N.Y.)

Billy Evans, Toledo 1932, 1949–1951. (Photo reprinted with permission of *The Toledo Blade*)

MIKE MARSHALL is foremost among former Mud Hens for having an impact on the major league record book, and became the first relief pitcher to win the Cy Young award as his league's best pitcher in 1974. Marshall owns the records for most appearances by a pitcher in both major leagues having 90 with the Minnesota Twins in 1979 and a phenomenal 106 with the 1974 Los Angeles Dodgers. Also in 1974, he set the major league record for innings pitched in relief in a season with 208. In addition to his iron man seasons, Marshall maintained his durability over a 14-year major league career, quite long for a relief pitcher. Marshall was a starting pitcher with the Mud Hens from 1967 through 1969 and was part of the outstanding staff that led Toledo to its only pennant of the Maumee Era in 1968. He is joined by two other former Mud Hens who have won the Cy Young award, Willie Hernandez (also a relief pitcher) of the Detroit Tigers in 1984 and Frank Viola of the Minnesota Twins in 1988. (Photo reprinted with permission of *The Toledo Blade*.)

EARL WEBB played in 162 games as an outfielder for Toledo over the 1924 and 1925 seasons, batting .330. He moved on to a major league career that saw him play for five different teams in seven seasons, and was not particularly distinguished. He did, however, become one of a number of former Mud Hens to set a significant major league record. With the Boston Red Sox in 1931, he slammed 67 two-base hits, a record that still stands. (Robert Koehler.)

HAL TROSKY hit 33 home runs in 1933 for the Mud Hens to eclipse the all-time mark of 24 which had been set by Erve Beck way back in 1899. His Toledo record stood until Jerry Witte smashed 46 in 1946 for the brood. The good, all-around player hit at a .323 clip that year, and was promoted to Cleveland for the next season. The slugging first baseman became an instant Indian star by batting a solid .330 and hitting 35 home runs and driving in 142 runs to establish rookie major league records. He also established rookie records, for extra base hits with 89 (45 doubles, 9 triples, and the 35 home runs), and for total bases with 374, that still stand. (Photo reprinted with permission of *The Toledo Blade*.)

Hal Trosky, Toledo, 1933. Note the closeness of the photographer. (Photo reprinted with permission of *The Toledo Blade*.)

At age 32, **SAM JETHROE** became the oldest rookie of the year in major league history. He did it playing for the Boston Braves in 1950. His record still stands. The veteran of six seasons in the Negro National League was signed by the Dodger organization and played two seasons at Montreal in the International League, just after Jackie Robinson. At Montreal he set the league mark for stolen bases with 89 in 1949. He was traded to the Braves and became the first black man to play in Boston, and led the National League in steals his first two seasons there. Jethroe was a Hall of Fame caliber player who was caught in the transition to the integrated game, and developed eyesight problems that cut short his major league career. (Photo reprinted with permission of *The Toledo Blade*.)

Frank Gilhooley, known as "Flash" for his speed, is shown here (on the right) with New York Yankee teammate and Hall of Famer Frank "Home Run" Baker. Gilhooley is one of 28 native Toledoans to go on to play in baseball's major leagues. The complete list follows with each player's debut year and the number of major league seasons played: Erve Beck (1899, 3); Roger Bresnahan (1897, 17); Stan Clarke (1983, 6); Rollin Cook (1915, 1); Dick Drago (1969, 13); Nig Fuller (1902, 1); Frank Gilhooley (1911, 9); Jack Hallett (1940, 6); Terry Harmon (1967, 10); Mickey Heath (1931, 2); Jesse Hoffmeister (1897, 1); George Kelb (1898, 1); Dennis Kinney (1978, 5); Merlin Kopp (1915, 3); Bill Laskey (1982, 6); Len Madden (1912, 1); Ollie Marquardt (1931, 1); Tom Marsh (1992, 3); Dan Masteller (1995, 1); Len Matusek (1981, 7); Bob Meyer (1964, 3); Doug Mientkiewicz (1998, 5); George Mullin (1902, 14); Ernie Neitzke (1921, 1); Jerry Nops (1896, 6); Ron Rightnowar (1995, 1); Al Schulz (1912, 5); and Ernie Vick (1922, 4). (Frank Patrick Gilhooley, Jr.)

After three seasons, 1933–1935, in Toledo, **STEVE O'NEILL** went on to manage 14 seasons in the major leagues, which included leading the Detroit Tigers to a World Series win over the Cubs in 1945. Thirty-seven other former Mud Hens have joined Steve O'Neill as major league managers and some rank among the best ever. Eleven have managed ten or more big league seasons: Casey Stengel (25), Joe McCarthy (24), Chuck Tanner (17), Tom Kelly (16), O'Neill (14), Billy Southworth (13), George Stallings (13), Fred Hutchinson (12), Al Buckenberger (10), Fred Haney (10), and Bill Terry (10). McCarthy ranks number five and Stengel number eight on the career wins list. Nobody has a higher career winning percentage than McCarthy. Southworth ranks fifth in that category while O'Neill and Terry rank in the top 20. In terms of championships, former Mud Hens as major league managers have won 35 pennants and 23 World Series. All three New York teams were managed by ex-Mud Hens for three consecutive years (1934 through 1936); McCarthy with the Yankees, Stengel with the Dodgers, and Terry with the Giants. (Robert Koehler.)

RALPH ELLIOTT LIN WEBER, shown here in 1988 at his home and baseball research office, literally wrote the book on early Toledo baseball history. He was the founder of the country's first baseball research library, the Baseball Research Bureau, in 1938. Lin Weber was

recognized by the Society for American Baseball Research with the SABR Award in 1986 for his "contributions to baseball knowledge and record keeping over a spectrum of many years." In 1944, he published *The Toledo Baseball Guide of The Mud Hens, 1883–1943*, a model baseball history and the definitive history of professional baseball in Toledo to that point. He was a contributing editor to the *Official Encyclopedia of Baseball* beginning in 1951, and is credited with identifying and documenting the first black player in the major leagues, Toledo catcher Moses Fleetwood Walker. Mr. Lin Weber was born in Rossford and was a lifelong Toledo area resident. He died in 1997. (Photo reprinted with permission of *The Toledo Blade*.)

ALL-TIME (1883–2002) ROSTER OF PLAYERS & INDEX

Roster includes players with a game appearance and are noted by year(s) played. Included are nineteenth century, Negro Leagues, twentieth century class C, American Association, and International League. Index notations are in parenthesis.

Brueggemann, Steve 1980 (86)
Brumley, Mike 1989
Bruner, Lawrence 1898
Bruno, Tom 1977
Brunsberg, Arlo 1967-70 (83)
Brunson, Will 1999
Buchanan, George 1935
Bucher, Jim 1942-4 (57)
Buckels, Gary 1995
Buckenberger, Al 1885 (118)
Buckeye, Garland 1928-9 (43)
Buckner, Jim 1979
Buffington, Lester 1922
Bullas, Sim 1884
Buller, Sean 2001
Bunning, Jim (77,103,113)
Bunson, Will (95)
Burck, Arthur 1907
Burgo, Bill 1944 (59)
Burke, Frank 1914 (34)
Burke, Les 1932
Burket, Harley 1883
Burns, Farmer 1900
Burns, Jack 1937
Burns, James 1885
Burns, John 1902,4
Burns, Otto 1910-3 (32,33)
Burr, Lefty 1923
Burris, Paul 1954-5
Burtt, Dennis 1985-6,90
Bush, Joe 1927 (40)
Bush, Paul 1914
Bush, Randy 1980,2 (86)
Bushelman, Jack 1908-9
Buskey, Tom 1977
Butcher 1929
Butera, Sal 1978-9
Butland, Bill 1949-50
Butler (27)
Butler, Ike 1899-1900
Butler, John 1903
Butler, Johnny 1930
Butler, Kid 1910-2
Buttle, Thomas 1914
Byrnes, Milt 1940-2
Cable, Harold 1917
Cadahia, Aurelio 1981
Caffrey, Robert 1926-7 (39)
Cage, Wayne 1977
Cahill, John 1914
Cain, Les 1968-71 (83)
Callahan, Dave 1910
Cally, Louis 1918
Calvey, Jack 1934-6
Camnitz, Howie 1905-6 (27)
Camp, Howie 1919
Campbell, Dave 1967-9 (83)
Campbell, Paul 1950-1
Campbell, Ray 1944
Camper, Cardell 1976-7
Campion, John 1892
Canavan, Hugh 1924-6
Cangelosi, John 1992-3
Cann, Mike 1912
Cannell, Rip 1906
Cannizzaro, Chris 1967 (83)
Caponigro, Joe (83)
Cardona, Javier 1998,2000-1
Carey, Scoops 1918
Cargo, Bobby 1901
Carisch, Fred 1911-2
Carlson, Vance 1952
Carlyle, Ken 1993-5
Carmichael, Dick 1954
Carney, John 1894-5
Caro, Jack 1954
Carpenter, Paul 1918

Carrasco, Norman 1989
Carrick, Bill 1903
Carroll, Doc 1914
Carroll, Frank 1916
Carroll, Ownie 1930
Carson, Kit 1936
Carter, Blackie 1928
Carter, Spoon 1939
Carter, Steve 1992
Casanova, Raul 1996-9
Cash, Frank 1930
Cash, Ron 1973
Casino Park (17)
Cassaday, Harry 1905
Castillo, Marty 1986
Castillo, Tony 1992
Castino, Vince 1946-7
Catalanotto, Frank 1997-8
Cates, Eli 1898-1900
Cates, Steve 1974
Caughey, Wayne 1978-9
Cave, Paul 1955
Cavelle, Charles 1895
Cerin, Jack 1952-3 (71)
Cernich, Joe 1969
Cerone, Rick 1976
Chamberlin, Buck (86)
Chambers, John 1927
Chambers, White 1926-7
Chandler, Ron 1967,9-70 (83)
Chapman, Ray 1911-2 (32,103)
Charleston, Oscar 1939
   (103,109)
Chauncey, K.C. 1981
Chavez B., Lupe 1975
Chavez, Pedro 1987-8
Chech, Charles 1906-7 (28)
Checo, Robinson 1999 (95)
Cherry, Joe Bobby 1968
Cherry, Paul 1988
Chiffer, Floyd 1985
Childs, Cupid 1901
Childs, James 1905
Childs, Pete 1903
Chipman, Bob 1953 (71)
Chism, Tom 1980 (86)
Christensen, Joe 1981-2
Christenson, Larry 1974-5
Christian, Bob 1968 (83)
Christian, Mark 1940-2
Christiansen, Clay 1986
Christopher, Jerry 1939
Christopher, Mike 1994-6
Cipot, Ed 1981
Claire, Danny 1921-2
Clark, Dad 1892
Clark, Otie 1949-50
Clark, Phil 1990-2
Clark, Rickey 1970
Clark, Ron 1974-5
Clark, Royale 1904-5 (27)
Clark, Tony 1994-6,99-2000
Clarke, Garry 1952
Clarke, Harry 1901
Clarke, Horace 1965
Clarke, Josh 1905-7 (28)
Clarke, Nig 1921
Clarke, Stan 1968 (117)
Clarke, Wilkie 1909
Clarke, William 1906-7 (28)
Clarkson, Bill 1926
Clarkson, Bus 1939
Clary, Ellis 1946-8
Clay, Danny 1986
Clayton, Schley 1920
Clements, John 1936
Clifford, Art 1970

Clifford, Thomas 1896
Clifton, Flea 1936-7 (50)
Clingman, Billy 1904-6 (27)
Clynes, John 1911
Cobb, Ty (28)
Cobley, Jim (53)
Coffman, Slick 1937,49 (50)
Coggswell, Charles 1902-3
Cogswell, Phil 1944
Cohen, Alta 1934-7 (51)
Colbert, Rick 1986
Cole, Ed 1940
Coleman, Dave 1979
Coleman, Ed 1937-8 (51,53,54)
Coleman, Paul 1970
Coles, Darnell 1987
Coletta, Chris 1974
Coley 1923
Collamore, Allan 1912-3,6,9
   (32,33)
Collier, Orlin 1935
Collins, George 1923
Collins, Kevin 1972-3
Collins, Ray 1921
Collins, Steve 1945
Comer, Wayne 1966-8,71-3
   (64,83)
Comstock, Keith 1984
Comyn, Bob 1944-5
Confrey, Bernard 1914
Congalton, Bunk 1912 (32)
Conlan, Jocko 1930
   (103,104,111)
Conley, Gene 1953
   (71,72,73,82)
Connally, Sarge 1930-1
Connaughton, Frank 1904
Connell, Truman 1938
Connelly, Bill 1949-52
Connolly, Bud 1926-7
Connor, Jim 1894-5
Connors, Edward 1903
Conway, Jack 1951
Cook, Gene (7,77,85,86)
Cook, Lewis 1888
Cook, Paul 1885
Cook, Rollin (117)
Cooke, Fred 1896 (19)
Coombs, Cecil 1918
Cooney, Johnny 1931
Cooper, Dave 1988-90
Cooper, Don 1982
Cooper, Wilbur 1926 (39)
Coquillette, Trace 2001
Corbett, Jim 1897
Corbett, Sherm 1992-3
Corbett, Stan 1938 (4,53)
Corey, Bryan 1999 (95)
Cornejo, Nate 2001-2 (98)
Corona, George 1943-9 (59,64)
Corrigan, Larry 1978
Cortazzo, Jess 1928
Cosma, John 1914 (34)
Cote, Pete 1926-7 (39,40)
Cotton, Bill 1973
Cotton, John 1996
Coughlin, Nathaniel 1903-4
Covert, William 1896
Covington, Wes 1955
Cox, Bill 1940,2-3 (57)
Cox, Eugene 1903
Cox, Larry 1974-5
Coyle, Bill 1896 (19)
Cradel, Ricky 1999 (95)
Craghead, Howard 1932-3
Crandall, Jim 1945
Crane, Mark 1975

Crawford, Patrick 1928
Creel, Jack 1949
Cregg, David 1913
Crevenstene, George 1914
Criscola, Tony 1940-1,3 (57)
Crist, Don 1945
Cristall, Bill 1903-4
Croft, Harry 1902
Cromley, Tate 1908
Crone, Ray 1954-5
Crossin, Frank 1917
Crossman, Harry 1914
Croucher, Frank 1937,46 (51)
Crow, Dean 1997-8
Crowe, George 1954 (94)
Crowley, Bill 1888
Crowley, Joseph 1910
Crum, Cal 1913 (33)
Crutchfield, Jimmie 1939
Cruz, Deivi 1998
Cruz, Fausto 1996
Cruz, Ivan 1991,3-5
Cruz, Jacob 2002
Cruz, Nelson 1999-2000 (95)
Cruz, Todd 1974
Cullen, Jack 1965-6
Cullenbine, Roy 1937-8 (54)
Culver, George 1974-5
Cummings, John 1997
Cummings, Steve 1991-2
Curry, Al 1935-6
Curtain, J.R. 1921
Curtis, Jack 1965-6
Cushman, Ed 1883, 9-90 (15)
Cuyler, Milt 1989-90,4-5
Dace, Derek 1997
Dailey, Sam 1935
Dalton, Mike 1991
Dammann, Bill 1895
Dancy, Bill 1975
Danielly, Paul 1923-4
Daniels, Jack 1953-5 (71,75)
Darby, George 1897 (19)
Darling, Dell 1892
Darwin, David 1998,2000
Dashner, Lee 1913 (33)
Datz, Jeff 1989
Daubert, Jake 1909
Daugherty, Doc 1951
David, Andre 1982-6 (90)
Davidson, Mark 1986
Davies, Thomas 1923
Davis, Alonzo 1903
Davis, Harry 1934,6
Davis, Jerry 1987
Davis, Jody 1990
Davis, Lomax 1952
de los Santos, Luis 1991
Deagle, Benjamin 1884
DeBarr, Dennis 1972,7
Decillis, Dean 1990-2
Decker, Claude 1921
Deering, John 1904
DeFreites, Arturo 1976
Deininger, Pep 1904
DeJesus, Ivan 1988-9
DeLaGarza, Alex 1950-1 (67)
Delli Carri, Joe 1995
DeLucia, Rich 2001
DeMontreville, Gene 1905-7
   (27)
DeMott, Ben 1912
Dempsay, Adam 1988
Dempsey, Lee 1923
Dempsey, Pat 1986
DeNeff, Jim 1970
Denehy, William 1971

Dennard, Dick 1945
Dennis, Bert 1914 (34)
DeNoville, Thomas 1918
Derrick, Claud 1920-1
Derrick, Frederick 1911-2 (32)
Derrick, Mike 1968-9 (83)
Desautels, Gene 1934
DeSilva, John 1991-3
Detore, George 1933
Devine, Jim 1888
Devine, Mickey 1918
DeVogt, Rex 1913,6 (33)
DeVormer, Al 1928-32
DeWald, Charlie 1892
Dewitt, Eddie 1923
Didier, Bob 1973
Diehl, Ernie 1907-8
Dietz, Dutch 1939
DiLauro, Jack 1967-8 (83)
Dillard, Don 1967 (83)
Dillinger, Bob 1941-2
DiLoreto, Dan 1933
DiMascio, Dan 1989
Diorio, Ron 1974
Dishman, Glenn 1997
Dobson, Pat 1967 (83)
Dochterman, Marcellus 1888
Doljack, Frank 1933
Doljack, Joe 1933-5
Donabedian, Harry 1952
Donahue, Jerry 1971
Donahue, Pat 1911
Donaldson, John 1971
Donnell, Clarence 1896
Donnelly, Charles 1917 (35)
Donovan, Fred 1909
Donovan, Mitchell 1904
Dooner, Glenn 1981-2
Dorn, Peter 1900,3
Doty, Babe 1890
Douglas, Steve 1980 (86)
Downs, Gil 1965-6
Doyle, Bob 1946
Doyle, Jack 1905
Doyle, Jess 1929
Drago, Dick 1967-8 (83,117)
Drews, Matt 1997-9 (95)
Drischell, Benjamin 1888 (63)
Driscoll, John 1903
Drumright, Mike 1997-9
Dubiel, Monk 1953-4 (71)
DuBois, Brian 1989-90
Dubuc, Jean 1920
Duck, Martin 1888
Duffy, John 1988
Dukes, Tom 1965
Dukes, Tommy 1939
Duncan, Pete 1923
Dunn, Cecil 1938-9 (53)
Dunn, John 1888
Duran, Roberto 1998
Durham, Bull 1911
Durham, Leon (98)
Durning, Rich 1919
Durrett, Isaac 1905 (27)
Dusan, Gene 1976
Dwyer, Double Joe 1939-40
Dwyer, William 1894
Dyer, Ben 1920-1
Dygert, Jimmy 1913
Earl, Scott 1987,9
Easley, Damion 2000,2
Eckenstahler, Eric 2002 (98)
Eckhardt, Ox 1938
Edinger, Don (71)
Edington, Stump 1913
Edmonds, Carl 1935-6

Edwards, Dave 1978
Edwards, Doc 1965
Edwards, Wayne 1994
Eells, Harry 1907-8 (28)
Eggert, Charles 1897
Eissick, William 1910
Eissler, Bill 1931
Elder, George 1947
Elliott, Rowdy 1924
Ellis, William 1912
Elwert, William 1908-10
Ely, Bones 1892
Embree, Red 1952
Encarnacion, Juan 1998
Engle, Dave 1979-80,2 (86,87)
English, Gil 1936
English, Woody 1925-6 (39)
Epler, Gus 1911
Epps, Hal 1943 (57)
Erickson, Roger 1979
Erie SeaWolves (97)
Ermer, Cal (77,86,89)
Ertman, Hank 1953 (71)
Escalera, Nino 1952 (70)
Espinoza, Alvaro 1984-6
Essian, Jim 1974
Essick, Bill 1911
Estalella, Bobby 1941
Estes, Doc 1979-81
Estock, George 1953-4 (71)
Eufemia, Frank 1985-6
Evans, Bart 2000
Evans, Billy (103,114)
Evans, Bob 1939
Evans, Steve 1916-7 (35)
Evans, Tom 2001
Ewing Street Park (17,18)
Ewing, Bob 1897-1900 (19)
Faatz, Jay 1885
Fabrique, Bunny 1917 (35)
Faedo, Lenny 1981
Falk, Bibb 1932 (52)
Falkenberg, Cy 1912 (32)
Fannin, Cliff 1943-5 (59)
Faraci, Joe 1966
Faries, Paul 1998
Farmer, Ed 1974
Farmer, Tom 2002
Farr, Jamie (77,85)
Farrell, Bert 1906
Farrell, John 1996
Faulkner, Ken 1966
Fayad, John 1945
Federoff, Al 1950-1
Felderman, Marv (63)
Felix, Paul 1988
Felton, Terry 1978-81,3 (103)
Ferens, Stan 1947
Ferguson, Alex 1919,29-31
Ferguson, Charlie 1896-9 (19)
Fermin, Ramon 1997
Fernandez, Frank 1966,73
Feron, Bob (71)
Ferraro, Mike 1966
Fick, Robert 1999-2000
Field, Greg 1978,84
Fields, Bruce 1987 (98,99)
Fiene, Lou 1905,11
Fifth Third Field (97,102)
Figner, George 1923
Filson, Pete 1982-3
Fink, Herman 1944
Finn, Mique (27)
Finneran, Happy 1923
Fisher, Clarence 1930
Fisher, Frank 1972
Fisher, Fritz 1967 (83)

Fisher, Gustavus 1908-9
Fisher, Harry 1901
Fisher, Nev 1897-8
Fitzgerald, John 1953-4
Flaherty, John 1994
Flanagan, Steamer 1902-3
Flannery, Kevin 1983
Fleming, Les 1939
Fletcher, Tom 1967-8
Flick, Elmer 1911-2 (103,109)
Flick, Lew 1944
Flippen, Conrad 1939
Florie, Bryce 1998,2001
Flournoy, John 1903
Flowers, Wes 1936
Fluhrer, John 1916-7 (35)
Fogg, Floyd 1950
Foldenauer, Carl 1939
Foley, Doc (83)
Foor, Jim 1971-2
Ford, Curt 1991
Ford, Russ 1917 (35)
Fore, Dave 1972-3
Foreman, Frank 1894
Forest Cemetery (104)
Fort Miami Fairgrounds (77,80)
Foster, Edward 1909
Foti, Tony 1949
Foulks, James 1905
Fournier, Jack (57)
Foutz, Frank 1901-2
Fox, Raymond 1920
Foytack, Paul 1951
Frank, Charlie 1894
Frank, Ed 1902,6
Franklin, Micah 1996
Frankovitch, Mitchell 1937
Fraser, Willie 1993
Freeman, Jeremiah 1909-10
Freeman, Lavel 1990
Fregin, Doug 1982
Freigau, Howard 1929 (43)
Fremming, Ken 1950-1 (67)
Fremuth, Mike 1970
French, Don 1937
Frensley, Jim 1970
Frey, Benny 1923-7 (39)
Frey, Jim 1955
Frisbee, Charlie 1904
Fritz, Larry 1974-5
Fritz, Ray 1936
Frost 1920
Frost, Jack 1911-2
Fryman,Travis 1990
Fulk, Bill 1967-70 (83)
Fuller, Nig 1907 (117)
Fullis, Chuck 1928
Fulton, Ed 1994
Funderburk, Arnold 1942
Funderburk, Mark 1981,6
Funk, Ernie 1951
Furman, Alan 1920
Fussleman, Les 1954
Gaffney, Thomas 1928
Gagne, Greg 1983-4
Gaillard, Eddie 1997 (93)
Gakeler, Dan 1991-2
Galasso, Bob 1977
Galatzer, Milt 1932-4
Gallagher, William 1895
Gallaher, Kevin 1996-7
Galle, Stan 1942,6
Gamble, John 1972-3
Gampher, Walter 1904
Ganley, Bob 1901
Garbark, Bob 1934-6
Garber, Gene 1974

Garcia, Karim 2000
Garcia, Leo 1989
Garcia, Luis 1998-9
Garcia, Nellie 1974,6
Garcia, Vince 1955 (75)
Gardiner, Mike 1993,5
Gardner 1923
Gardner, Earle 1912-3,6 (32,33)
Gardner, Vassie 1976-7
Garfield, Bill 1888-9
Garland, Lou 1936-7
Garver, Ned 1945
Gaston, Alex 1924-5
Gastright, Hank 1888
Gatch, Walter 1902
Gatewood, Bill 1923
Gatlin, Mike 1978
Gazarek, Marty 2001
Gehrig, Lou (42)
Gelbert, Charlie 1938 (53,54)
Gelnar, John 1971
Gentry, Rufe 1949
George, Augus 1903
George, Lefty 1912-3 (32)
Gerheauser, Al 1948
German, Franklyn 2002
German, Harry 1902-4
Gettinger, Tom 1892
Getz, Gus 1919
Geyer, John 1902
Geyer, Rube 1905
Giard, Joe 1922-4 (37)
Gibboney, Raymond 1914
Gibbs, Jake 1965
Gibson, John 1946
Gibson, Kirk 1987 (91)
Gibson, Paul 1987
Gibson, Ralph 1905
Giebell, Floyd 1939
Giegler, Mark 1973
Gilbert , George 1914
Gilbert, Andy 1946-7
Gilbert, Jack 1905
Gilbreth, Bill 1971-2
Gilhooley, Bob 1969-70
Gilhooley, Frank Patrick, Jr. (38,53,69,101)
Gilhooley, Frank Patrick, Sr. (38,117)
Gilks, Bob 1894-5,97-1902 (19,25,46)
Gill, George 1940
Gillen, Grover 1906-8 (28)
Gillespie, Eric 2000
Gilliand, Rusty (57,59)
Gilligan, Jack 1910
Ginsberg, Myron 1949-50
Giordano, Mike 1983
Girouard, Gary 1966
Givens, Jim 1993-5
Gladden, Dan 1993
Glidden, Sewell 1933
Gnadinger, Edwin 1901
Goar, Jot 1895
Goedde, Stretch 1943-5 (59)
Gohr, Greg 1991-6
Goldsmith, Gary 1997-9
Gomez, Chris 1993
Gomez, Henrique 1993
Gomez, Preston 1952
Gonzales, Frank 1992-5
Gonzales, Orlando 1976-7
Gonzales, Tony 1977
Gonzalez, Pete 1992,4-5
Gooden, Ernest 1923
Gordon, Herman 1923

121

Gorin, Charlie 1954-5
Gorinski, Bob 1978
Governor's Cup (82,89)
Grace, Joe 1939
Graffius, William 1901-2
Graham, Bill 1967
Graham, Dan 1978-9
Grant, Charles 1948
Grant, George 1925
Grapenthin, Dick 1989
Grater, Mark 1993
Graterol, Beiker 1999
Gray, Chet 1945
Gray, Pete 1946 (64)
Grayson, Tom 1971-2
Green, Daniel 1910
Green, Lenny 1967-8 (83)
Greenberg, Joe 1938 (53)
Greene, Rick 1997
Greenstein, Burton 1953
Gregory, John 1969-70
Gregory, Ken 1944
Gregory, Nick 1943 (57)
Greisinger, Seth 1998-9,2002
Gresham, Kris 1998
Griffin, Alan 1977
Griffin, Alfredo 1996-7
Griffin, David 1989
Griffin, Don 1951
Griffin, Stephen 1899-1900
Griggs, Art 1911-2
Grilli, Steve 1972-3
Grimes, Kenneth 1921
Grimes, Ray 1926 (39)
Grimes, Roy 1921-2,6-8
  (37,39,40,103)
Grissom, Marv 1950
Groh, Heinie 1926 (39)
Groom, Buddy 1991-5
Grossman, Bob 1977
Grubb, Harry 1952
Grube, Frank 1940
Grumbling, Frederick 1888
Gryska, Sig 1941
Grzanich, Mike 1999 (95)
Guerra, Rich 1977
Guettler, Ken 1952 (70)
Guevara, Giomar 2000-1
Guilfoyle, Mike 1996
Gullickson, Bill 1993
Gullman, Theodore 1921
Gutteridge, Don 1946
Haas, Bert 1912
Haas, Bruno 1931
Haas, Dave 1991-3
Hadding, Louis 1903
Haggerty, Pat 1951
Haines, Leslie 1921
Hairston, Napoleon 1939
Hajek, Dave 1997
Hale, Odell 1932
Hall, Drew 1994
Hall, Irvin 1947
Hall, Joe 1995,7
Hallett, Jack (117)
Hallman, William 1910-1
Hamby, Jim 1928
Hamelin, Bon 1997,9
Hamilton, William 1917
Hammond, Don 1923
Hammond, Jack 1921
Hamner, Grant 1948
Hanaford, Charles 1900
Hancken, Buddy 1938 (53,54)
Hancock, Garry 1977
Hancock, Raymond 1910
Handrahan, Vern 1970

Hanebrink, Harry 1953-5
Haney, Fred 1935-8
  (51,53,54,56,118)
Hanna, John 1885
Hannah, Shawn 2001
Hannahs, Gerry 1981
Hanning, Loy 1942-3,8 (57)
Hannivan, Jimmy 1904
Hansen, Mike 1989-90
Hansen, Terrel 1996
Hare, Joe 1936-7
Hare, Shawn 1990-4,7 (64)
Hargan, Steve 1978
Harmon, Charlie (70)
Harmon, Terry (117)
Harriger, Denny 1997-8
Harrington, Mickey 1965
Harris, Billy 1978
Harris, Bob 1938,46 (53,54)
Harris, Gene 1994
Harris, Joe 1901
Harris, Vic 1939
Harris, William 1910
Harrison, Roric 1978
Harshaney, Sam 1941,6
Hart, Hub 1911
Hart, Mike 1981,3-5
Hart, Walter 1914 (34)
Hartley, Grover 1910
Hartman, Fred 1895
Hartman, William 1896-1900
  (19)
Hartsel, Topsy 1912-4 (32,34)
Hartzell, Roy 1917 (35)
Harvey, Bill 1939
Harvin, Al 1932
Hassamaer, Bill 1897 (19)
Hassey, Ron 1977
Hatfield, Gil 1894
Hatter, Clyde 1937 (51)
Hauger, Arthur 1911-3
Havens, Brad 1983-4,9 (89)
Hawley, Scott 1895
Hayes, Buddy 1923
Hayworth, Ray 1929
Hayworth, Red 1943 (57)
Hazelton, Doc 1904
Healey, Francis 1933
Healy, John 1890
Heams, Shane 2000-1
Heath, Bill 1967
Heath, Mickey (117)
Hecht, Steve 1995
Hegan, Jim (81)
Hegan, Mike 1965-6 (81)
Heimach, Fred 1930
Heimueller, Gorman 1986
Heinkel, Bob 1987-8
Heise, Bob 1976
Heismann, Crese 1902
Helf, Hank 1947
Helgeth, Bernard 1924
Hemsley, Rollie 1952
Henderson, Benjamin 1913
Henderson, Craig 1985
Henderson, Curt 1939
Hendricks, John 1885
Henges, Harvey 1914
Henline, Butch 1930-3
Henneman, Mike 1987
Hennessey, Joseph 1902
Henriquez, Oscar 2002 (98)
Henry, Dwayne 1995-6
Henry, George 1894
Hensley, Eggie 1923
Herbert, Raymond 1949-50
Herbst, Frank 1922

Herbst, Kelly (47)
Herman, Babe 1937 (51)
Hermann, Ibert 1926 (39)
Hernaiz R., Jesus 1974-5
Hernandez, Fernando 1997
Hernandez, Toby 1985
Hernandez, Willie 1975,87
  (91,115)
Herrera, Jose 1971
Herschler, Herbert 1924
Hersh, Earl 1954
Herz, Steve 1980-1 (86)
Heving, Johnnie, 1926-7
  (39,40)
Hiatt, Phil 1996 (63,93,94)
Hickman, Charlie 1908-11 (31)
Higginbotham, Irv 1911-2
Higginson, Bobby 1994,6
Hiljus, Erik 1999-2000
Hill, Alan 1920-2 (37)
Hill, Lewis 1888
Hill, Quency 1975
Hiller, John 1967 (83)
Hillis, Mack 1925
Hilton, Dave 1977
Hinchman, Harry 1907-12
  (29,31)
Hinkle, Gordie 1938 (54)
Hodge, Ed 1981-6
Hoeft, Billy 1951
Hoff, August 1901-2
Hoffer, Bill 1892
Hoffman, Danny 1903
Hoffman, Tex 1916
Hoffmeister, Jesse (117)
Hohnhorst, Eddie 1911-2
Hoiles, Chris 1988
Hoke, Bud 1945
Holbert, Ray 1997
Holdsworth, Fred 1972-3
Holland, Dutch 1934
Holland, Will 1894
Holly, Jeff 1979
Holman, Shawn 1989-90
Holmes, Ducky 1910
Holmes, Stan 1985-6
Holmes, Tommy (74)
Holmquist, Theodore 1909
Holsey, Tim 1972
Holt, Johnny 1923
Hooker, Bill 1904
Hoover, Dick 1953-5 (71,74)
Hopkins, John F. 1930
Hopkins, John W. 1908
Hord, Maurice 1896
Horsford, Jim 1965-6
Hosley, Tim 1971
Houk, Ralph (75)
House of David (47)
House, Frank 1951
House, Roy 1936,8 (53)
Houtz, Bill 1952
Howard, Doug 1976
Howe, Gregory 1985-6
Howell, Dixie 1936
Hruska, John 1926
Hubbard, Stanley 1918
Huber, Clarence 1921-2
Hudek, John 1993
Hudson, Charles 1989
Hudson, Roy 1932
Huff, Ken 1939
Hughes, Dick 1966
Hughey, Jim 1894-5,1901-2
Huismann, Mark 1988
Huizenga, John 1967
Hulsen, Jack 1942

Hulswitt, Rudy 1916
Humphrey, Clyde 1945
Hunnefield, Bill 1930
Hunter, Lem 1883
Huntzinger, Walt 1927-8
  (40,43)
Huppert, Dave 1981
Hurley, Jerry 1892
Hurst, Bill 1998
Hurst, Jimmy 1997
Hurst, Jody 1992-3
Hutchinson, Freddie 1939
  (118)
Hutt, Oscar 1923
Hyatt, Ham 1919
Hyers, Tim 1996-7
Ibarra, Jesse 1998
Ignasiak, Ed 1944-5 (58,59,60)
Infante, Omar 2002 (98)
Inge, Brandon 2000-2 (98)
Ingram, Riccardo 1992-4
Iorg, Dane 1974-5
Iott, Clarence 1946
Isaac, Lou 1977
Jackson, Bill 1934
Jackson, Darrell 1979,81-2
Jackson, James 1902
Jackson, Ryan 2001-2 (98)
Jacobs, Art 1925
Jacobs, Ray 1928
Jacobson, Baby Doll 1928
James, Bill 1910-2 (32)
James, Roy 1934-5
James, William 1911-3 (32)
Jamison, William 1885
Jansco, George 1936
Jarvis, Kevin 1997
Jata, Paul 1971-3
Jay, Joey 1955
Jefferies, Gregg 1999
Jefferson R. 1945
Jeffries, Irv 1930
Jenkins, Alban 1900
Jenkins, Fats 1939
Jensen, Marcus 1997
Jeric, Frank 1945
Jester, Virgil 1953-4 (71,74)
Jeter, Derek (69)
Jethroe, Sam 1953 (71,73,117)
Jimenez, Elvio 1965-6
Jimenez, Houston 1982-3,5
Johnson, Ben 1954-5
Johnson, Brian 1997
Johnson, Chet 1946-8
Johnson, Craig 1998,2000
Johnson, Dave 1992-3
Johnson, David C. 1978
Johnson, Dicta 1923
Johnson, Earl 1998
Johnson, Fred 1923-6,37-40
  (54)
Johnson, Jack 1939
Johnson, Jimmy 1939
Johnson, Johnny 1938-9 (53,54)
Johnson, Mark 2000-2
Johnson, Milo 1950
Johnson, Randy 1983-4
Johnston, Greg 1980-1 (86)
Johnstone, Jay 1974
Jones (43)
Jones, Bob 1940
Jones, Charlie 1913 (33)
Jones, Davy 1913
Jones, Earl 1943-4,6-7 (59)
Jones, Guy 1928
Jones, Jack 1883 (11)
Jones, Jeff 1987 (98)

Jones, John 1919-20
Jones, LeRoy 1930
Jones, Samuel (24)
Jonnard, Claude 1925
Jordan, Brian (95)
Jordan, Buck 1928
Jordan, Milt 1951
Joss, Addie 1900-1
  (24,103,107)
Joyce, Bill 1889
Jude, Frank 1906
Jurewicz, Mike 1966
Just, Joe (71,74)
Kaiser, Al 1945
Kaiser, Jeff 1991-2
Kaiserling, George 1916
Kalafatis, George 1970-1
Kalita, Tim 2002 (98)
Kane, Frank 1919
Kane, Harry 1903
Kane, William 1900-1
Kapler, Gabe 1999 (95)
Kapuscinski, Ted 1950
Kaufman, George 1945
Keagle, Greg 1996-9
Keane, Willis 1906
Kearns, Tom 1885
Kearse, Jeff (98)
Keating, Ray 1917 (35)
Keenan, Kid 1896-8 (19)
Kelb, George 1896-7 (19,117)
Keller, Ardys 1942-3 (57)
Keller, Kris 2001-2 (98)
Kellogg, Bobby 1952 (70)
Kellum, Win 1905
Kelly, Bernard 1920
Kelly, Bryan 1987
Kelly, Joe H. 1919-20
Kelly, Joe J. 1927 (40)
Kelly, Mike 1918-20
Kelly, Owen 1923-5
Kelly, Tom 1978 (118)
Kemmer, Bill 1904 (27)
Kendrick, Harry 1969-70
Kenna, Ed 1900
Kent, Ed 1884
Kerns, Russ 1952-3 (71)
Kerr, Buddy 1953-4 (71)
Kersey, Gil 1934
Ketcham family (9)
Ketcham, George (15)
Ketcham, Valentine, Jr. (15)
Ketchum, Gus 1924
Kettler, John 1902
Kida, Masao 1999-2000
Kiely, John 1991-5
Kies, Norm 1930-1
Kiesel 1914
Kiger, Herbert 1935
Kihm, George 1896 (19)
Kilkenny, Mike 1968 (83)
Killen, Frank 1894
Kimball, Leighton1948
Kimberlin, Harry 1940-5 (59)
Kimble, Dick 1942-7
  (57,59,60)
Kimm, Bruce 1973
Kincannon, Harry 1939
King, Eric 1988,92
King, Lee 1922 (37)
Kinney, Dennis 1976-7 (117)
Kinnunen, Mike 1980-1 (86)
Kinsella, Bob 1924-5
Kinsella, Ed 1906
Kinzer, Matt 1990
Kirke, Jay 1913 (33)
Kirsch, Harry 1910

Kirton 1897
Kiser, Larry 1974-5
Kisinger, Rube 1901
Kitt, Howie 1965
Klaus, Billy 1953 (71,74)
Klawitter, Tom 1984
Klee, Ollie 1926
Kleinow, Red 1902-3
Kline, Bob (55)
Kline, Doug 1992
Kline, Steve 1976
Klinger, David 1928-9 (43)
Klobas, Rusty 1974
Knabe, Otto 1906
Knaupp, William 1917
Knickerbocker, Austin 1949-50
  (67)
Knickerbocker, Bill 1930-2
Knierim, Elwood 1945-6
Kniffin, Chuck 1974
Knisely, Pete 1919
Knoll, Julius 1902,4
Knox, Johnny 1972-3
Knudsen, Kurt 1991-4
Kocher, Brad 1922 (37)
Koehler, Pip 1926-31
  (39,40,43,46)
Kokos, Dick 1948
Komminsk, Brad 1997
Konetchy, Ed 1922 (37)
Koonce, Don 1973
Kopf, Larry 1912-3 (32)
Kopfshaw, George 1922
Kopp, Merlin (117)
Korczyk, Steve 1982-3
Kores, Art 1920
Korince, George 1967-70 (83)
Kosco, Andy 1975
Koslo, Dave 1954
Koster, Fred 1936
Kowitz, Brian 1996
Kramer, Jack 1940,3 (57)
Kramer, Tommy 1995
Krause, Harry 1912 (32)
Kromy, Ted 1982
Krueger, Bill 1993
Krueger, Ernie 1913
Krueger, Otto 1906
Kryhoski, Dick 1950
Kuhn, Charlie 1969-71,3
Kuhns, Frederick 1903
Kunkel, Jeff 1994
Kutcher, Randy 1991
Kwiatkowski, Terry (83)
Kynett, Roe 1914
Laabs, Chet 1937-8 (54)
Laabs, Frank 1921
LaFleur, Floyd 1914
Laga, Frank 1950
LaGrow, Lerrin 1971-3
Laguna, Ted 1955
Lally, Dan 1897
LaMacchia, Al 1944-5 (59,64)
Lamar, Bill 1918,21-4 (36,37)
Lamb, Lyman 1923
Lambe, Bryan 1973
Lamont, Gene 1970
Land, Grover 1905-10,2-3
  (28,32)
Landrum, Jesse 1940
Lane, Chappy 1883-4 (11,12)
Lane, George 1914
Lane, Marvin 1973
Lanfersieck, Ed 1945 (60)
Langsford, Bob 1897 (19)
Lape, William 1914
Larkin, Steve 1934

Lasher, Fred 1967 (83)
Laskey, Bill 1987 (117)
Lasko, Bob 1996,9
Laskowski, Rudy 1935
Laskowski, Walt 1934-5
Latham, Bill 1986
Lattimore, Bill 1907-9 (28,29)
Laudner, Tim 1982
Lawlor, John 1904
Lawrence, Michael 1901
Lawson, Roxie 1932-5
League Park (11,12,17)
Leake, Albert 1913
LeBourveau, Bevo 1926-7,30-1
  (39,45,48)
Lee, Mark 1988
Lee, Sidney 1914
Lee, Thornton 1932-3
Lee, Watty 1904-5 (27)
Leek, Randy 2000-1
Legg, Llewellyn 1888
Leggatt, Rich 1986
Lehner, Paul 1946
Lehnhardt, Milt 1939
Leiper, Tim 1988-90,5
Leipsic 1900
Leiter, Mark 1991
Lemanczyk, Dave 1972-3
Lemonis, Chris 2000
Lenardson, William 1888
Lennon, Pat 1999 (95)
Leon, Rich 1972-3
Leonard, Red 1935-6
Lerchen, George 1949-51
Leshnock, Don 1972
Leslie, Sam 1930
Lewis, Bert 1924
Lewis, Herman 1952
Lewis, Jim 1983
Lewis, Richie 1996
Lima, Jose 1994-6 (68,92)
Lin Weber, Ralph (58,104,118)
Lind, Carl 1927
Lindeman, Jim 1990
Linderbeck, Albert 1904
Lindley, John 1929
Lindsey, Rod 2002
Lindstrom, Axel 1929
Lindstrom, David 1998,2000-1
Lindstrom, Freddie 1922-3
  (37,103,108)
Link, Bobby 1989-90
Linnert, Tom 1976
Linton, Bob 1936-8 (53)
Lira, Felipe 1993-4,9
Lis, Joe 1976-7
Lister, Pete 1908
Little, Jeff 1982-3
Little, Keith 1949
Littleton, Larry 1982
Litzsinger, Norb 1946
Livingston, Paddy 1912-3
Livingstone, Scott 1990-1
Lloyd, Harry 1900
Lober, Elmer 1921
Lobmiller, Paul 1919
Lockwood, Horace 1883 (11)
Lollar, Tim 1987
Lomastro, Jerry 1984-6
Lombardo, Lou 1949
Lombardozzi, Steve 1984-5,90
Lonchar, John 1978
Long, Dennis (9)
Long, Harry 1907
Long, Herman 1904
Long, Herral (76)
Looney, Brian 1999 (95)

Lopez, Art 1965-6
Lopez, Junior 1967-8,70-1 (83)
Loucks, Harry 1905 (27)
Loux, Shane 2001-2 (98)
Love, Andy 1945
Lovelace, Vance 1992
Lovullo, Torey 1988-90
Lowry, Dwight 1987
Luby, Pat 1894
Lucadello,Johnny 1940,51
Lucas County Recreation
  Center (80,81, 92,96)
Lucas, Jim 1946
Lucas, Ray 1929 (43)
Luderus, Fred 1921-2
Lugo, Urbano 1990
Lukachyk, Robert 1995
Lumley, Mike 1993
Lund, Don 1949-51 (67)
Lund, William 1888
Lundbom, Jack 1902,4-5
Lupien, Tony 1949
Lusader, Scott 1987-90
Lutz, Barney 1946
Lyden, Mitch 1991
Lynch, Michael 1909
Lyon, Russ 1945
Lyons, George 1925-6
Lysander, Rick 1984-5
MacArthur, Mac 1885
MacCormack, Frank 1977
Machemer, Dave 1980-2
Macias, Jose 1999-2000 (95)
Mackie, Vern 1939-40
MacPherson, Bruce 1979-81
  (86)
Madden, Bill 1966-7
Madden, Edward 1898
Madden, Len (117)
Madden, Morris 1987
Madrid, Sal 1948
Magee, Wendell 2000-1
Maguire, Freddie 1924-7
  (39,40)
Main, Miles 1916
Mains, Jim 1945,7
Mainzer, Bob 1953
Majtyka, Roy 1965
Makarewicz, Scott 1997
Makowski, Tom 1972-3
Malloy, Marty 2000
Malone, Pat 1922-3
Maloney, Billy 1911
Manassau, Albert 1894
Mancuso, Frank 1948
Mangham, Eric 1991
Manion, Clyde 1921
Mantick, Dennis 1979
Mantilla, Felix 1954-5 (75)
Mantle, Mickey (69)
Manuel, Jerry 1973
Manush, Frank 1912
Manush, Harry 1921
Mapel, Steve 1980-2
Marberry, Firpo 1937-8 (54)
Marcan, Lily 1903
March, Ed 1949-50
Marcum, Johnny 1940-2,6
Marentette, Leo 1967-9 (83)
Marine, Del 1998
Marlow, Ed 1934
Marlowe, Dick 1950-1
Maroth, Mike 2001-2 (98)
Marquardt, Ollie (59,117)
Marquez, Luis 1953-5
  (71,73,75)
Marriott, William 1927-8 (40)

123

Marsh, Tom (117)
Marshall, Mike 1967-9 (83,115)
Marshall, Randy 1991,5-6
Marte, Alex 1986
Martel, Ed 1995
Martin, Babe 1944-7 (59)
Martin, David 1904-5
Martin, James 1896
Martin, Jerry 1974-5
Martinez, Pedro 1998
Martinez, Romulo 1999
Marting, Tim 1969-71
Martz, Tom 1966
Mashore, Justin 1995
Massalsky, Bill 1945
Matchick, Tom 1967 (83)
Mathews 1888
Matthews, Jack 1923
Matusek, Len (117)
Maun, Ernie 1926-8 (39,40)
Mavis, Bobby 1949-50 (67)
Maxcy, Brian 1994-6
Maxwell, Jason 1999 (95)
May, Dave 1978
Mayo, Eddie 1949
Mays, Carl 1930-1 (32)
Mays, Willie (69)
McAleese, Dan 1905
McCain, Mike 1983
McCarthy, Joe 1908-11 (103,107,118)
McCartney, Steve 1975
McCarty, Dave 1999 (94,95)
McCarty, John 1919
McClain, Boots 1923
McClure, Brian 2000
McColl, Alex 1916,8-21
McConnell, Art 1950
McCormick, Mike 1912 (32)
McCoy, Benny 1937-9 (53,54)
McCullough, Frank 1924
McCullough, Paul 1921-2,4,6-8 (37,39,40)
McCurdy, Harry 1929 (43)
McCurry, Jeff 1996
McCutchin, Jim 1976
McDill, Allen 2000
McDonald, Jim 1885
McDonough, Jeremiah 1897-9 (19)
McDougall, Art 1940
McDowell, Ward 1913
McElhone, Thomas 1888
McFarland, Ed 1894 (63)
McGill, William 1903
McGinnis, Edward 1896
McGloughlin, William 1923
McGough, Tom 1977
McGowan, Edward 1896
McGraw, Jim (45)
McGrew, Alvin 1975
McGriff, Terry 1995
McGuckin, Joe 1894
McGuire, Deacon 1884 (12,103)
McIntyre, Harry 1901
McKain, Archie 1942
McKeel, Walt 1999 (95)
McKenzie, Pete 1970
McKillen, Mutt 1913
McKinley, Edward 1901
McKinley, Samuel 1911
McLaughlin, James 1883
McLaughlin, Pat 1938-9 (53)
McLeland, Wayne 1951

McMahon, Don 1955
McMahon, John (39)
McMahon, Thomas 1888
McMillan, Thomas 1925
McMillan, Tom 1976
McMillon, Billy 2000 (96)
McNamara, Tim 1926,8-9 (39,43)
McNaughton, Harold (35)
McNeal, Harry 1902
McNeil, Norm 1920
McNichol, George 1897
McQuillan, Hugh 1929-30
McQuillen, Glenn 1940-1, 1947-8,51-2
McRae, Norm 1969-70
McSorley, Trick 1884
McSurdy, Daniel 1909
Meacham, Rusty 1991
Mead, Henry 1920-1
Meade, Dick (27,39)
Meaney, Patrick 1902
Mee, Julian 1922
Meeks, John 1918
Meeks, Sammy 1955 (75)
Meeler, Phil 1972-3
Meier, Dave 1983
Meis, Carl 1925
Meister, George 1884 (12)
Meloan, Paul 1911-2
Melson, Gary 1977
Mendenhall, Kirk 1994-5
Mendez, Carlos 2000-1
Menendez, Danny (70)
Meoli, Rudy 1979
Meran, Jorge 2001-2
Meredith, Richard 1901
Meridith, Ron 1987
Merkle, Fred (14,26)
Merrick, Raphael 1922
Merritt, ED 1955-6
Mesa, Ivan 1982
Messner, Glenn 1928
Metcalf, Tom 1965
Metz, Lenny 1925
Meusel,Irish 1927
Meyer, Bob (117)
Meyers, Bert 1902
Meyers, Ed 1935
Meyers, George 1923
Meyers, Leonard 1905
Michel, Domingo 1989-90
Middleton, Jim 1920
Middleton, Roxy 1912
Mientkiewicz, Doug (117)
Mikkelsen,Pete 1965
Miles, Edward 1896
Miles, Willie 1923
Miljus, Johnny 1919
Miller, Bill 1938
Miller, Donald 1914
Miller, Dusty 1894, 1901-2
Miller, Ed 1884
Miller, Joe 1883-4 (11,12)
Miller, John 1966
Miller, Matt 2001
Miller, Orlando 1997
Miller, Ox 1944-6 (59)
Miller, Pearl 1904,7
Miller, Richard 1888
Miller, Trever 1996
Miller, William 1897,1901
Mills, Jack 1912
Milnar, Al 1947
Milne, Darren 1995
Milstead, George 1927-8 (40)
Minahan, Cotton 1905-6

Minor, Ray 1948
Missler, Walt 1944-5 (59)
Mitchell, Bobby 1982,4
Mitchell, Charlie 1986-7
Mitchell, Mike 1902
Mitchell, Tony 1996-7
Mitchell, Willie 1912
Mlicki, Dave 2000
Mock, Homer 1902-3
Moehler, Brian 2001-2
Moffet, Joe 1884
Moffet, Sam 1883 (11)
Moher, Art 1949
Molinaro, Bob 1972-3
Molush, Ed 1975
Monroe, Craig 2002 (98)
Montag, Bob 1953 (71,74)
Montague, Ed 1933-4
Moon, Leo 1932
Moore, Ansel 1952
Moore, Archie 1965-6
Moore, Dave 1980
Moore, Edward 1928-9 (43)
Moore, Ernest 1914
Moore, Jim 1932
Moore, Robert 1914
Moore, Roy 1936
Moore, William 1930
Moran, Al 1965
Mordarski, Ed 1949-51 (67)
Moreton, Red 1904
Morgan, Barry 1969-70
Morgan, Charles 1921
Morgan, Chet 1935,7-8 (51,53)
Morhardt, Greg 1986
Moriarty, George 1904-5 (27)
Morney, Leroy 1939
Morris, Barney 1939
Morris, Jim 1939
Morris, Robert 1951
Morrisette, Bill 1921
Morrison, Jon 1885
Morton, Charlie 1883-4,9 (9,11,12,13,15,84)
Moss, Les 1946
Mostil, Johnny 1930-1
Moulder, Herb 1941
Mouton, Lyle 2001
Moyer, Jamie 1992
Mud Hen (17,66,80)
Mud Hen, Mortimer (66)
Mud Hen, Muddy (95,101)
Mueller, Heinie 1928
Mullane, Tony 1884 (9,12,14,63)
Mulleavy, Gregory 1929-31
Mullen, Charlie 1917 (35)
Muller, Freddie 1939
Mulligan, Bob 1883-4
Mullin, George (117)
Mullin, John 1898
Mundy, John 1928
Munoz, Mike 1991
Munson, Eric 2002 (98)
Murcer, Bobby 1966 (81)
Murphy, Dick 1952
Murphy, Dwayne 1988
Murphy, Ed 1905
Murphy, Frank 1922 (37)
Murphy, James 1919-20,2 (37)
Murray, Ed 1919
Murray, Heath 2001
Murray, Jed 1987
Murray, Mitch 1923
Myers, 1913
Myers, Bade 1987-9 (19)
Myers, Hy 1926

Myers, Mike 1995
Nagelsen, Lou 1912
Nagelson, Russ 1970-1
Nagle, James 1908-9
Nahorodny, Bill 1975
Nalbock, Charles 1927 (40)
Nally, Alvin 1909
Nance, Doc 1905-6
Napier, Joseph 1925
Napoli, Joe (100)
Nash, Ken 1913
Naylor, Rollie 1924-5
Ned Skeldon Stadium (92,102)
Nedelco, Alex 1951-2
Needham, Tom 1914
Neighbors, Bob 1940
Neighbors, Cy 1905
Neitzke, Ernie (117)
Nekola, Bots 1933-4
Nelson, Bill 1885
Nelson, Byron (56)
Nelson, Emmett 1937-9 (53,54)
Nelson, Luke 1920
Nettles, Morris 1976
Neun, Johnny 1929 (43)
Neville, Eddie 1950-1
Nevin, Phil 1995,7
Newell, John 1892
Newlin, Maury 1946
Newman, Jeff 1975
Newman, Jesse 1941
Nichol, Sam 1892
Nicholas, Jeff (83)
Nichols, Chuck 1914 (34)
Nichols, Ed 1935
Nicholson, Derek 2002
Nicholson, Fred 1923-5
Nicholson, Parson 1889-90,2
Niekro, Joe 1972-3 (68)
Nigro, Alexander 1931
Niland, Tom 1894-5
Niles, Harry 1911-2 (32)
Nill, Rabbit 1909
Nitkowski, C.J. 1996,2001
Noessel, Conrad 1970
Nops, Jerry 1895 (117)
Nordquist, Herb 1941
Norrid, Tim 1976
Norris, Jim 1976
Norwood, Willie 1980
Nosek, Randy 1989-91
Nothe, Walter 1949
Novick, Walter 1952
Nunez, Edwin 1989
O'Brien, Frederick 1905
O'Brien, Jerry 1888
O'Brien, Joseph (39)
O'Brien, Syd 1973
O'Brien, William 1896
O'Connell, John 1898
O'Connor, Jack 1982-4
O'Day, Hank 1883-4 (11,12,14,104)
O'Dea, Paul 1946
Odwell, Fred 1906
Oelkers, Bryan 1983,5
Ogden, Curly 1930
O'Hara, Bill 1904-5 (27)
Okrie, Bob 1945 (60)
Okrie, Frank 1920-1
Olin, Frank 1884 (12)
Olivares, Omar 1996
Oliver, Dave 1976-7
Oliver, Rick 1976
Olivo, Federico 1955
Olympic Park (17)
O'Neil, Ed 1890

O'Neil, Mickey 1927-8 (40)
O'Neill, Charles 1923
O'Neill, Steve 1932-4 (48,118)
O'Neill, William 1921-3
Onis, Butch 1936
Oquist, Mike 2000
O'Reilly, Tom (55)
O'Rourke, Frank 1888
Ostermueller, Fritz 1942
Ostrowski, Joe 1948
Otis, Harry 1910
Ouellette, Phil 1990
Overmire, Stubby (83)
Owen, Frank 1909-10
Owens, Red 1902-3
Pacella, John 1987-8
Pack, Frank 1945
Page, Leonard 1924
Paige, Pat 1911
Paine, Phil 1954
Palacios, Rey 1987-8
Palmer, Dave 1989
Palmer, Dean 2001
Palmer, Donald 1948
Palmero, Emilio 1927-30
  (40,43)
Paniagua, Jose 2002
Pardee, Alfred 1901-2
Paredes, Johnny 1991-3
Parker, Clay 1990
Parker, Harry 1976
Parker, Harry R. 1888
Parker, Salty 1935-6
Parker, Tom 1939
Parkinson, Frank 1926
Parks, Jack 1954
Parks, Slicker 1922,9
Parmelee, Roy 1927-9,41-2
  (40,43)
Parrish, Lance 1994
Parrot, Ray 1942,6
Parsil, Robert (66)
Parsons, Dixie 1939
Parton, James 1950
Pashnick, Larry 1984
Patchin, Art 1937
Patterson, Danny 2002
Patterson, Daryl 1967 (83)
Patterson, Floyd 1929
Patterson, Jarrod 2001-2 (98)
Patton, William 1914
Paul, Mike 1974-5
Pavelko, Paul 1968-70
Pavlick, Jr., John 1945-7
Pawlicki, Irv 1933
Payne, Bob 1947
Paytan, Armand 1940
Peak, Elias 1888
Pears, Frank 1892
Pearsey, Les 1980 (86)
Pearson, Monte 1932-3
Pearson, Terry 2002
Pechous, Charlie 1922-3
Pecord, Ollie 1892,4
Pederson, Alfred 1935
Pedrique, Al 1989
Peel, Homer 1938
Pegues, Steve 1991
Peltz, John 1890
Pemberton, Rudy 1994-5
Pena, George 1972
Pena, Hipolito 1992
Pena,Ramon 1987-9
Pendleton, Jim 1955
Pendry, John 1914 (34)
Penn, Shannon 1994-6
Penny, Robert 1952

Pepper, Don 1967-8 (83)
Perez, Jhonny 2001
Perisho, Matt 2001-2 (98)
Perlozzo, Sam 1978
Perme, Len 1949
Perna, Andy "Doc"
  (53,54,57,59)
Perrin, Bill 1934
Perring, George 1907,16 (28)
Perry, Bill 1935
Perry, Boyd 1939
Persails, Mark 2001
Perzanowski, Stan 1976,8-9
Peters, Rusty 1948
Peterson 1914
Peterson, Sid 1943,5 (57)
Petoskey, Ted 1939
Pettibone, Jay 1983-4
Pettis, Gary 1989,92
Petty, Charlie 1895
Pettyjohn, Adam 2000-1
Pevey, Marty 1992-3
Pfeffer, Jeff 1926-9 (39,40,43)
Pfiester, Jack 1902
Phelps, Tommy 2001
Phillips, Bubba 1951
Phillips, Milton (39)
Phillips, Red 1939
Piatt, Wiley 1905-6
Piatzke, Oliver 1914
Pick, Charlie 1910-1
Piechota, Al 1950
Pierce, George 1916
Piercy, Bill 1917
Piggott, John 1883
Pike, Charles 1988
Pinciotti, Gabriel (80,104)
Pineda, Luis 2001
Pinhey, Lon (95)
Pinkney, Frank 1909
Pittaro, Chris 1986
Pittinger, Pinky 1931
Pittman, John 1978
Platt, Whitey 1947
Poeppleman, Ralph 1922
Poffenberger, Boots 1938
Poinsette, Robert 1939
Pokorney, Edward 1907 (28)
Pollard, Bentley 1896
Polly, Nick 1945
Polonia, Luis 1999 (95)
Poole, Ralph 1951
Poole, Stine 1983
Poorman, Tom 1883-4 (11,12)
Popp, Bill 1901
Portugal, Mark 1985-6
Powell, Bill 1952 (70)
Powell, Brian 1998,2002 (98)
Powell, Hosken 1979
Powell, Roger 1945
Powers (43)
Powers, Mike 1932-7 (48,51)
Presque Isle Park (17)
Price, Samuel 1883
Pride, Curtis 1996
Prince, Walter 1894
Pritchard 1896
Prpish, Paul 1944
Pruiett, Tex 1908
Pruitt, Ron 1977
Przybycien, Tony 1966
Puckett, Kirby 1984 (103,110)
Pugh, Tim 1997
Purtell, Billy 1918
Pyle, Ewald 1939,42
Pytlak, Frankie 1932
Queen, Billy 1953-5 (71,73,75)

Quest, Joe 1889 (15)
Quinn, Jack 1908
Rabb, William 1928-32 (43)
Radatz, Dick 1968 (83)
Rafferty, John 1888
Rafferty, Tom 1909
Raich, Eric 1976-7
Rainey, John 1885
Ralston, Bobby 1986
Rambone, Paul 1953 (71)
Ramirez, Alex 1979
Ramirez, Jose 1999
Ramirez, Mario 1986
Ramos, Jose 1990
Ramsey, Bill 1952
Randall, Bobby 1980
Raney, Ribs 1943,6-8
Rankin, Matt (98)
Ransom, Jeff 1987
Rapp, Goldie 1924
Rapp, William 1911
Rawlings, Johnny 1916,28
Reading, Charles 1904
Reagan, Stephen 1907 (28)
Reams, Leroy 1970
Redfern, Buck 1929
Redfern, Pete 1978
Redman, Mark 2001
Redmond, Wayne 1967,9,70
Redys, Ed 1946
Reed, Billy 1953-5 (71,74)
Reed, Bob 1967-72 (64,83)
Reed, Brandon 1998-2000 (95)
Reed, Jeff 1983-6
Reeder, Icicle 1888
Reel, Jimmy 1923
Reese, John 1923
Reiber, Frank 1933,7
Reid, Earl 1948
Reid, Jackie 1939
Reimink, Bob 1992-3
Reims 1914
Reinhart, Fred 1944-5 (59,60)
Reis, Bobby 1933-4
Reisling, Doc 1903-4
Repoz, Roger 1965
Restaino, Emil 1950 (67)
Rettger, George 1894
Reynolds 1914
Reynolds, Bob 1976
Reynolds, Jeff 1988
Reynolds, Ken 1977
Rhawn, Bobby 1952
Rheas 1934
Rhiel, Bill 1933
Rhodes, Leon 1932
Rice, Lance 1995
Rice, Pete 1988
Richardson, James 1930-1
Richardson, Marty 1968-9 (83)
Richbourg, Lance 1920
Richie, Rob 1989
Richmond, Don 1948
Richmond, Lee (113)
Ricketts, Dave 1965
Riebe, Harvey 1950
Righetti, Leo 1952
Rightnowar, Ron 1990-3 (117)
Riley, Jim 1912-3 (32)
Ring, Jimmy 1929 (43)
Rios, Brian 2001-2 (98)
Ripken, Billy 1998
Ripplemeyer, Ray 1954-5
Ritchie, Wally 1993
Ritter, Floyd 1890
Ritter, Jack 1954
Ritter, Reggie 1988

Ritz, Jim 1894
Ritz, Kevin 1989-91
Rivera, German 1987
Rivera, Homero, 2002
Rivera, Lino 1990
Rivera, Mike 2000,2
Riverside Park (17)
Roach, Mike 1895
Roach, Peter 1999
Roberts, Bip 1998
Roberts, Dale 1966
Roberts, Willis 1998-9 (95)
Robertson, Jerry 1970
Robertson, Rod 1992-3
Robinson, Humberto 1955
Robinson, Jackie (13,117)
Robinson, Jeff 1992
Robinson, Jim 1946
Robinson, Karl 1909-11
Robinson, Smokey 1973
Robinson, Zeke 1902
Roderick, Barry 1977
Rodgers, William 1914 (34)
Rodney, Fernando 2002
Rodriguez, Adam 1997
Rodriguez, Andy 1976-7
Rodriguez, Steve 1996-7
Roettger, Oscar 1935
Rogalski, Joe 1938-9 (54)
Rogers, Chuck 1980
Rogers, Edgar 1910
Rogers, Emmett 1889-90
Rogodzinski, Mike 1974-5
Rogovin, Saul 1950
Rohr, Bill 1970-1
Rohr, Jim (86)
Rojek, Stan 1952
Roman, Bill 1965
Romero, Ramon 1986
Roof, Gene 1987 (95)
Rooker, Jim 1967-8 (82,83)
Rosario, Victor 1991-2
Rosenfeld, Max 1929-30
Rosengren, John 1997
Roskopf, George 1914
Ross, Buck 1948
Ross, Don 1936-7
Routcliffe, Phil 1888
Routson 1900
Rowelley 1888
Rowland, Donnie 1988
Rowland, Rich 1990-3
Roxbury, Joe (53)
Ruble, Art 1929,31
Rudd, Emery 1947-8
Ruffin, Leon 1939
Ruiz, Benny 1988
Runge, George 1918
Runyan, Sean 1999-2001
Russell, Rip 1949
Ruth, Babe (38,42,74)
Ruthven, Dick 1975
Ryan, Rosy 1926-8,31
  (39,40,42)
Sabel, Erik 2002
Sabota, Andy 1939
Sackett 1914
Saferight, Harry 1974,82
Sage, Harry 1889-90 (15,16)
Sager, A.J. 1996,8
Sain, Tommy 1979
Salazar, Oscar 2002 (98)
Sales, Ed 1888
Sallee, Slim 1922
Salm, Walter 1902
Sanchez, Alex 1986
Sandate, Rich 1975

125

Sanders, Reggie 1972-3
Sanders, Roy 1918-9
Sands, Charlie 1973
Sanford, Fred 1942-3,6 (57)
Santana, Blas 1974-5
Santana, Julio 2002 (98)
Santana, Marino 1998
Santana, Pedro 2001
Santiago, Ramon 2002
Santorini, Al 1974
Santos, Henry 1995
Santos, Victor 1998,2000-1
Sarmiento, Wally 1980-1 (86)
Sasser, Rob 2000
Saunders, Dennis 1970-1
Sawhill, William 1888
Scanlan, Bob 1996
Scanlon, Michael 1901
Scarce, Mac 1974,8
Schaeffer, Harry 1954
Schafley, Lawrence 1901
Schaub, Robert 1903
Schaufele, Alexander 1921-2
Scheer, Albert 1916
Scheibeck, Frank 1890,1902
Scherman, Fred 1968-9 (83)
Schills, Bert 1900
Schliebner, Dutch 1924-6
Schlitzer, Biff 1913
Schmakel, Jim (83)
Schmidt, Bob 1965-6
Schmitt, Todd 1998
Schmitz, Danny 1983-4
Schneck, Dave 1975
Schoof, Carl 1933
Schroeder, Casper 1896
Schrom, Ken 1983
Schubert, Lester 1925
Schulte, Johnny 1924-5
Schulte, Len 1943-4,6 (57,59)
Schultz, Carl 1942,7
Schultz, Joe 1944 (59)
Schultz, John 1911
Schulz, Al 1917-8 (35,117)
Schulze, Don 1988
Schwabe, Mike 1989-90
Schwamb, Blackie 1948
Schweitzer, Al 1918
Scott, Bill 1946-7,9
Scott, Everett 1927 (40)
Scott, Hobart 1933
Scott, Jack 1924,8,30-1
Scott, Kelly 1935
Scott, Lee 1965
Scrivener, Chuck 1971-3
Scudder, Dan 1940
Scweitzer, Albert 1918
Searcy, Steve 1987-90 (90)
Sebesak, George 1944
Secory, Frank 1939
See, Larry 1989
Seelbach, Chuck 1970-1,3
Seibert, Kurt 1980-1 (86)
Seiger, Benny 1914 (34)
Seinsoth, Bill 1943-4 (57,59)
Selkirk, George
   (69,71,73,74,84)
Sellers, Rick 1933
Selway, Ed 1938
Senger, Charlie (83)
Sertich, Mike 1944
Serum, Gary 1979-80 (86)
Sewell, Rip 1934
Sexton, Tom 1885
Seybold, Socks 1909
Seydler, Arthur 1922-4
Shafer, Tom 1965

Shaffer, Taylor 1889 (15)
Shank, Waldo (21,53,56)
Shanklin, Robert 1923-4
Shannon, Joseph 1923-4
Shantz, Bill 1966
Sharkey, Thomas 1914
Sharon, Dick 1973
Shaw, Albert 1916
Shaw, Don 1973
Shea, Andrew 1919
Sheehan, Terry 1979
Shelby, John 1990
Sheldon, Rollie 1969
Shelly, Hugh 1936
Shinners, Ralph 1922,4
Shires, Len 1934
Shirley, Tex 1947
Shoeberg, Ralph 1921
Shoffner, Milt 1931
Shore, Ray 1947
Shoup, William 1922
Siddall, Joe 1998-9 (95)
Silber, Eddie 1940
Silicato, Tom 1974
Simon, Randall 2001
Simons, Mel 1931
Simpson, Halbert 1950
Simpson, Wayne 1975
Siner, Emil 1914
Singleton, Duane 1996
Sinovic, Dick 1954
Skeldon, Ned (7,77,92,96)
Skeldon, Sue (92)
Slagle, Walt 1898
Slapnicka, Cy 1911
Slayback, Bill 1972-3
Sleater, Lou 1955
Sloat, Lefty 1949-51 (69)
Smalling, Earl 1945-6
Smith, Al 1939
Smith, Burt 1954
Smith, Carlos 1905 (27)
Smith, Don 1944-5 (59,60)
Smith, Earl 1930
Smith, Elmer 1913 (33)
Smith, Frank 1885
Smith, Fred 1889-90 (15)
Smith, Greg 1992
Smith, Hal 1930
Smith, Harry 1923
Smith, Ira 1997-8
Smith, John 1927-31
Smith, Jud 1902
Smith, Leroy 1986
Smith, Melville 1897,1901
Smith, Myrl 1978
Smith, Oscar (39)
Smith, Ray 1979-80,2,4 (86)
Smith, Red (72,74)
Smith, Roy 1944
Smith, Rufus 1928
Smith, Theodore 1908
Smith, Theolic 1939
Smith, Tommy 1976
Smith, William 1896-1900,3
   (19)
Smoll, Lefty 1936
Smoot, Homer 1907-9 (28)
Sneed, John 1889-90 (15)
Snell, Nate 1987
Snider, Kelly 1981-2
Snyder, Bill 2000
Snyder, Frank (65)
Sodders, Mike 1982
Soderholm, Dale 1978
Sodowsky, Clint 1995-6
Sofield, Rick 1978-9,81-2

Soherbarth, Elmer 1922
Solomini, Ron 1965
Solomon, Mose 1924-5
Solt, Jim 1953 (71)
Somers, Charlie (21,28,30,34)
Sorce, Sam 1984,6
SoRelle, Ben 1940-1
Sorrell, Vic 1937-8 (53)
Southworth, Billy 1913
   (33,118)
Sparks, Greg 1992
Sparks, Steve 2000
Sparma, Joe 1971
Spatz, Gene 1972-3
Speece, Byron 1927 (40)
Spence, Don 1944
Spence, Stan 1952 (70)
Spencer, Chet 1908
Spencer, Pee Wee 1939,45
Spencer, Raymond 1913
Speranza Park (15,17)
Spicer, Keith 1971-3
Spikes, Charlie 1977
Spindel, Hal 1940-2 (55)
Sprague, Charlie 1889-90
Springer, Steve 1994-5
St. Pierre, Maxim 2002
Stafford, Bill 1966
Stahlman, Dick 1931
Staker, Bill 1945
Stallings, George 1889 (15,118)
Stanfield, Kevin 1978-9
Staton, Joe 1972
Stearnes, Turkey 1945
   (103,110)
Stearns, John 1974
Stebbins, George 1914
Steen, Bill 1908
Stein, Irv 1935-6
Steinbacher, Hank 1940-2
Stemmyer, Bill 1885
Stengel, Casey 1926-9,31
   (21,39,40,41,42,43,46,47,69,
   103,104,118)
Stenhouse, Mike 1987
Stephens, Vern 1941
Stevens, Chuck 1941-2,7
Stevens, Frank 1923
Stevenson, Lester 1913
Steverson, Todd 1995
Stewart, Joe 1904
Stidham, Phil 1994
Stis, Charles 1909
Stitzel, Glenn 1974
Stoker, Don 1954
Stokes, Art 1921
Stone, Eric 1990
Stone, Jeff 1992
Storti, Lin 1941-4 (57)
Stovall, George 1916
Stover, Dewey 1928
Strahler, Mike 1973
Straker, Les 1986
Strampe, Bob 1972-3
Strand, Paul 1916,24-5
Strange, Doug 1987-9
Strickland, Jim 1976
Stricklett, Elmer 1900
Strief, George 1888
Strobel, Charles
   (7,10,19,24,84)
Strothers, John 1888
Stroughter, Steve 1981
Strueve, Al 1888
Stryker, Sterling 1920
Stuart, Marlin 1948-50 (68)
Stumpf, Bill 1913 (33)

Sullivan 1898
Sullivan, Bill 1944 (59)
Sullivan, Dennis 1910
Sullivan, Edward (40)
Sullivan, Joe 1937
Sullivan, Lefty 1935-6
Sullivan, Russ 1951
Summers, Tack 1923
Summers, William 1894
Sunday, Art 1889
Sundra, Steve 1934
Susce, George 1935
Sutthoff, John 1906-8 (28)
Sutton, John 1978
Swann, Oscar 1911-2
Swann, Pedro 1998-9 (95)
Swanson Karl 1930
Swanson, Chip 1971-3
Swartwood, Ed 1890
Swayne Field
   (11,21,28,30,31,38,39,
   44,52,61,62,68,76,102)
Swayne, Noah (11,21,30,38)
Sweeney, Bill 1904
Sweeney, Bill 1932-3
Sweeney, Ed 1916-7 (35)
Sweeney, Hugh 1914 (34)
Sweeney, James 1928-31 (43)
Swindell, Josh 1913
Szotkiewicz, Ken 1971-2
Tackett, Jeff 1995-6
Talbot, Bob 1955
Talbot, Richard 1912
Talbot, Robert 1901
Tanner 1888
Tanner, Chuck 1953 (103,118)
Tate, John H. 1939
Tate, John P. 1929-31 (43)
Taylor, Candy Jim 1923
Taylor, Ed 1928-9 (43)
Taylor, Fred 1952
Taylor, Gary 1969-71
Taylor, Harry 1939-40
Taylor, Johnny 1939
Taylor, Kerry 1998
Taylor, Robert 1900
Taylor, Zack 1940 (56)
Teague, Clarence 1913 (33)
Teasley, Ron 1945
Tebeau, George 1890
Tebeau, Bill 1922-3
   (37,103,106,118)
Teufel, Tim 1982-3 (88)
Thayer, Greg 1978-9
Thiel, Bert 1953-5 (71,74,75)
Thomas, Fay 1926
Thomas, Herb 1929 (43)
Thomas, Myles 1935 (53,54)
Thomas, Oliver (53)
Thomas, Red 1935-6
Thomas, Reggie 1995
Thomas, Roy 1974-5
Thomason, Erskine 1974-5
Thompson, Arthur 1883
Thompson, Blackie 1945-6 (60)
Thompson, Bobby 1977
Thompson, Frank 1920
Thompson, Glenn 1953-5 (71)
Thompson, Justin 1996
Thormodsgard, Paul 1978-9
Thorpe, Bob 1954
Thorpe, Jim 1921 (36)
Tiburcio, Fred 1987
Tiefenauer, Bob 1965
Tighe, Jack (77,83,84)
Tighe, Tom 1939
Tilley, John 1883-4 (11)

Timmerman, Tom 67-71,4
(64,83,83)
Todtenhausen, Art 1967,9,70
(83)
Tolar, Kevin 2000-1
Toledo Black Pirates (7,9,15)
Toledo Blue Stockings
(7,9,11,14)
Toledo Bresnahens (35)
Toledo Crawfords (22)
Toledo Cubs (22)
Toledo Exhibition Company
(38)
Toledo Glass Sox (72)
Toledo Holding Company (39)
Toledo Iron Men (7,21,35)
Toledo Maumees (7)
Toledo Mud Hens
(7,17,19,21,34,77,97)
Toledo Soumichers (7,34)
Toledo Sox (7,22,72,97)
Toledo Swamp Angels (7,10)
Toledo Tigers (22)
Toledo Toledos (7,12)
Toledo White Stockings (7,9)
Tolman, Tim 1987
Tomberlin, Andy 1998
Tomkinson, Phil 1953
Torcia, Tony 1969
Torpe, Dom 1925-6
Torre, Frank 1955 (75,103)
Torres, Andres 2002 (98,99)
Torreyson, Thayer 1896
Toth, Paul 1965-6
Trail, Chet 1966
Trammell, Bubba 1996-7 (94)
Treadway, Charles 1938 (54)
Treadway, Ted 1939
Tresh, Mike 1936-7
Tri State Fairgrounds (12)
Trosky, Hal 1932-3 (63,94,116)
Trout, Dizzy 1937-8 (48,53)
Trowbridge, Bob 1955
Truby, Chris 2002
Trujillo, Mike 1988-9
Tunnell, Lee 1995
Tunney, James 1925-6
Turgeon, Pete 1931-4
Turner, Etwood 1923
Turner, Ted 1914,9 (34)
Turner, Tuck 1900-3
Twogood, Forrest 1932-3
Uhle, George 1934
Ullger, Scott 1982,4-6
Ulrich, Henry 1936
Underwood, Tom 1974
Urban, Luke 1926-7 (39)
Urbani, Tom 1996
Valera, Yohanny 2002
Valle, Hector 1969-71
Valliere, Bradley 1910-1
Van Dyke, Bill 1889-90 (15)
Van Dyke, Samuel 1914
Van Eman, Robert 1952
Van Giesen, Charles 1896,1901
Van Hekken, Andy 2002
Van Winkler, Arthur 1896 (19)
Vance, Dazzy 1917
(35,103,112)
Vangilder, Elam 1930-2
Veach, Bobby 1926-9
(39,40,41,43)
Vega, Jesus 1979-81,3 (86)
Verhoeven, John 1979
Veryzer, Tom 1973
Veselic, Bob 1980-2 (86)
Vesling, Don 1989-91

Vetters, Samuel 1896 (19)
Vick, Ernie (117)
Vickers, Rube 1900
Vickery, Lou 1965
Vico, George 1950 (67)
Vidal, Jose 1971
Viebahn, William 1911
Vigerust, Herman 1923-5
Villafuerte, Brandon 2000
Villalobos, Carlos 2000
Vilorio, Frank 1979
Vincent, Al 1936
Viola, Frank 1982 (115)
Viox, Reney 1902
Vukmire, Mike 1952 (70)
Vukovich, George 1988
Vukovich, John 1975
Wade, Gale 1955
Wade, Jake 1940
Wagener, Charles 1940
Wahl, Kermit 1954
Wakefield, Howard 1908
Wakeland, Chris 2000-2 (98)
Walbeck, Matt 1997,2002 (98)
Wales, Frank 1903
Walewander, Jim 1987-9
Walinski, Carl (44,45)
Walker, Bill 1928
Walker, Curt 1932
Walker, Dixie 1931
Walker, Edward 1903
Walker, Fleet 1883-4
(9,11,12,13,103,118)
Walker, Hub 1935
Walker, Jamie 2002 (98)
Walker, Jerry 1966
Walker, Johnny 1980-1 (86)
Walker, Mike 1992,6
Walker, Roy 1913
Walker, Welday 1884 (9,12,13)
Walkup, Jim 1938
Wall, Joe 1901
Wall, Murray 1953-4 (71,74)
Wallace, Don 1965
WallaceDave 1974-5
Walls, Doug 2000
Walsh, Augie 1935
Walsh, Jim 1921
Walsh, John 1888
Walsh, Walter 1912 (32)
Walters, Clyde 1914
Walters, Mike 1982-5
Ward, Aaron 1928
Ward, Chris 1977
Ward, Chuck 1924
Ward, Daryle 1996
Ward, Gary 1978-80 (86)
Ward, Jack 1931-2
Ward, Monte (113)
Ware, Bob 1971-2
Warner, Jack 1929-30 (43)
Warren, Brian 1993
Warren, Roxy 1913
Warthen, Dan (95)
Washer, Buck 1902
Washington,Ron 1980-1,6 (86)
Watkins, Pat 2000
Watkins, Robert 1914
Weafer, Ken 1935
Weaver, Floyd 1965
Weaver, Jeff 2000
Weaver, Jim 1984-5
Webb, Earl 1924-5 (115)
Webb, Lefty 1909
Weber, Jim (101)
Weddige, Albert 1895
Wedge, Eric 1996

Weeden, Bert 1911
Wehrle, William 1889 (15)
Weil, Edward 1925
Weiland, Bob 1929,30
Weinert, Phil 1934
Weintraub, Phil 1942-3 (57,61)
Weis, Butch 1936
Weiss, John 1951
Welch, Curt 1883-4 (11,12)
Welch, Tub 1890
Wells, Boomer 1982 (87)
Wells, Robert 1916-7
Wenig, Frederick 1904
Wenson, Paul 1989
Werber, Billy 1931
Werd, Norm 1976
Werden, Perry 1889-90 (15,63)
West, Dave (61)
West, Hi 1907-12 (28)
West, Max 1932-4
Westmoreland, Claude 1982
Weston, Mickey 1995
Wetherell, Delano 1931
Wetzel, William 1898
Wheeler, Don 1952
Wheeler, Ed 1898
Whillock, Jack 1970,2
Whinnery, George 1892
Whisenant, Pete 1954-5 (75)
Whitaker, Steve 1966
White, Derrick 1995
White, Fuzz 1946-7
White, Hal 1949
White, Harry 1932
White, Jack 1928
White, Robert 1923
Whitehead, John 1940-1,3-5
(57,59)
Whitehouse, Len 1984-5
Whitestocking Park (17)
Whitney, Pinky 1940
Whitted, Possum 1922-3 (37)
Whittmore, Reggie 1985
Wickander, Kevin 1995
Wickland, Al 1920-2 (37)
Wicks, Bill (37)
Wieligman, Rich 1988-9
Wiggs, Jimmy 1906
Wilburn, Chet 1938 (54)
Wild, George (32,33)
Wilder (27)
Wiley, Craig 1990
Wilhoit, Joe 1920
Willard, Glenn 1947
Willey, Carl 1955
William, Clyde 1907
Williams 1914
Williams, Al 1980,2,4 (86)
Williams, Big Jim 1939
Williams, Brian 1996
Williams, Chester 1939
Williams, Chief 1918
Williams, Clyde 1908 (28)
Williams, Dewey 1953 (71)
Williams, Errol 1913
Williams, Errol 1913
Williams, Harry 1939
Williams, Kenneth L. 1989
Williams, Kenneth R. 1989
Williams, Pete 1939
Williams, Raymond 1913 (33)
Williams, Rick 1981-2
Williams, Ted (69)
Williams, Ted 1993
Williams, Willie 1952 (70)
Wilson, Craig 1995
Wilson, Craig 2002 (98)

Wilson, Dan 1939
Wilson, Frank 1930
Wilson, Hack 1925 (103,113)
Wilson, Harvey 1939
Wilson, Jim 1948
Wilson, Mike 1922
Wilson, Tack 1983-4 (88)
Wilson, William 1904
Wiltse, Snake 1899-1900
Winegarner, Ralph 1932-3,40-1
(52)
Wingard, Ernie 1929-31,5
(43,63)
Wingfield, David 1923
Wirkkala, Les 1939-41
Wise, Harold 1916-19 (35)
Wise, Hughie 1932
Wisner, Jack 1927 (40)
Wissel, Dick 1947-5
Wissman, Dave 1967 (83)
Witte, Jerry 1946-7
(63,93,94,116)
Wolcott, Fred 1970-1
Wolf, Steve 1992
Wolgamot, Earl 1922
Womack, Dooley 1965
Wood, Jacob 1967
Wood, Jason 1998,9
Wood, Ken 1943,6
Wood, Roy 1916
Woodlawn Cemetery (38, 108)
Woodall, Larry 1920
Woodbury, Mitch (35)
Woodlock, Michael 1901
Woods, Al 1985-6
Woods, Gary 1977
Woods, Ron 1967-8 (83)
Woolfolk, Ernest 1923,5-7 (39)
Woyt, Butch 1948
Wren, Bob 1943-7 (57,58,59,60)
Wright, Bob 1921-3 (37)
Wright, John 1930
Wright, Johnny 1939
Wright, Ken 1974
Wright, Lucky 1909
Wright, Rasty 1885
Wright, Rasty 1929
Wright, Rick 1987
Yancy, Hugh 1976
Yantz, George 1917
Yaryan, Yam 1922
Yeager, George 1905 (27)
Yett, Rich 1984-5
Yingling, Earl 1909-11
Young, Cy (65)
Young, Delwyn 1988-9
Young, George 1913 (33)
Young, John 1972-3
Young, Kip 1982
Younker, Ralph 1939
Zachary, Chris 1972,4
Zahniser, Paul 1918-9,29
Zapor, Johnny 1938 (53)
Zapustas, Joe 1934-5
Zarilla, Al 1943
Zearfoss, Dave 1905
Zeider, Rollie 1919
Zepp, Bill 1971
Zesing, Oscar (33)
Zieser, Clarence 1952
Zinn, Guy 1910
Zinter, Alan 1994-5

BIBLIOGRAPHY

Bresnahan, Roger/Mud Hens Chapter of the Society for American Baseball Research. *Blue Stockings to Mud Hens*, Toledo, OH, 1998.

Britsch & Munger, Architectural Firm. *Projects Developed for Toledo and Lucas County Ohio*: Toledo and Lucas County Planning Commissions, 1943.

Carter, Craig ed. *Sporting News Complete Baseball Record Book*, St. Louis: The Sporting News, 2002.

Creamer, Robert W. *Stengel His Life and Times*, New York: Simon and Schuster, 1984.

Daniels, Robert. Unpublished manuscript.

Doyle, Pat. *The Professional Baseball Player Database*: Old Time Data, Inc., 1995–2000.

Holway, John. *The Complete Book of Baseball's Negro Leagues*, Fern Park FL: Hastings House Publishers, 2001.

Ivor-Campbell, Frederick. *Baseball's First Stars*, Cleveland, The Society for American Baseball Research, 1996.

Johnson, Lloyd & Miles Wolff, eds. *The Encyclopedia of Minor League Baseball*, Durham NC: Baseball America, Inc., 1997.

Lin Weber, Ralph Elliott. *The Toledo Baseball Guide of the Mud Hens 1883–1943*, Rossford OH: Baseball Research Bureau, 1944.

Lucas County, Ohio Recorder's Office. *Lease Records*.

Madden, W.C., & Patrick J. Stewart. *The Western League: A Baseball History, 1885 Through 1999*, Jefferson, NC: McFarland & Company, Publishers, 2002.

Riley, James A. *The Biographical Encyclopedia of the Negro baseball Leagues*, New York: Carroll & Graf Publishers, 2002.

Skipper, John C. *A Biographical Dictionary of the Baseball Hall of Fame*, Jefferson NC: McFarland & Company, Publishers, 2000.

The Society for American Baseball Research. *Minor League Baseball Stars*, Manhattan KS: AgPress, Inc., 1984.

The Society for American Baseball Research. *Minor League Baseball Stars Volume II*, Manhattan KS: AgPress, Inc., 1985.

The Society for American Baseball Research. *Minor League Baseball Stars Volume III*, Birmingham AL: EBSCO Media, 1985.

The Sporting News Guides, (1942-1955, 1966-2002)

Thorn, John; Pete Palmer; & Michael Gershman, eds. *Total Baseball*, Kingston NY: Total Sports Publishing, 2001.

The Toledo Bee

The Toledo Blade

The Toledo News-Bee

The Toledo Times

Wright, Marshall. *The American Association*, Jefferson NC: McFarland & Company, Publishers, 1997.

Zang, David W. *Fleet Walker's Divided Heart*, Lincoln NE: the University of Nebraska Press, 1995.